Shapland & Turner

Cases in Financial Accounting

FIRST EDITION

Shapland & Turner

Cases in Financial Accounting

FIRST EDITION

JULIA P. SHAPLAND
University of Illinois

CYNTHIA W. TURNER
University of Illinois

PEARSON

Boston Columbus Indianapolis New York San Francisco Upper Saddle River
Amsterdam Cape Town Dubai London Madrid Milan Munich Paris Montreal Toronto
Delhi Mexico City Sao Paulo Sydney Hong Kong Seoul Singapore Taipei Tokyo

Editorial Director: Sally Yagan
Editor in Chief: Donna Battista
AVP/Executive Editor: Stephanie Wall
Editorial Project Manager: Nicole Sam
Editorial Assistants: Jane Avery, Lauren Zanedis
Development Editor: Ginny Bess Munroe
Director of Marketing: Maggie Moylan Leen
Marketing Assistants: Ian Gold, Kimberly Lovato
Senior Managing Editor: Nancy Fenton
Production Project Manager: Alison Eusden
Senior Manufacturing Buyer: Carol Melville
Cover Designer: Anthony Gemmellaro
Media Project Manager: Sarah Peterson
Production Media Project Manager: John Cassar
Printer/Binder: Bind-Rite
Cover Printer: Bind-Rite

Credits and acknowledgments borrowed from other sources and reproduced, with permission, in this textbook appear on the appropriate page within text.

Photo Credits
p. 1, ©Hammondovi / iStockPhoto; **p. 23,** Jupiter Images / Getty Images; **p. 73,** © Image Source / Alamy; **p. 131,** © azndc / iStockPhoto

---

Cataloging-in-Publication Data is on file at the Library of Congress.

10 9 8 7 6 5 4 3 2 1

ISBN 10: 0-13-275281-6
ISBN 13: 978-0-13-275281-7

Table of Contents

1 Project DJ

2 Project Wedding Planner

Table of Contents

3 Project Orthodontist

Table of Contents

4 Project Movie Theater

About the Authors

Julia P. Shapland is a lecturer in accountancy at the University of Illinois in Urbana-Champaign. Julie graduated with highest honors from the University of Kentucky with a BS in accountancy and from the University of Illinois with a MS in taxation. Over the last 12 years, Julie has taught federal income taxation, intermediate accounting, as well as the introductory financial and managerial accounting sequence. Most recently her efforts have been focused on designing and teaching an innovative, large lecture, introductory accounting course that is required of most business majors. Julie is a proponent of team-based learning and accordingly utilizes realistic cases (that are carefully crafted for the introductory student) to provide what she believes is a deeper and more meaningful learning experience. Julie has been consistently recognized for her efforts in the classroom. She was recently awarded the "2010-2011 Heads Award for Teaching Excellence." Her students have also shown their appreciation; throughout her career, she has been honored to be included on the University of Illinois's "Incomplete List of Teachers Ranked as Excellent."

Prior to beginning her teaching career, Julie was a practicing accountant with the firms of Olive, LLP and KPMG, LLP where she served closely-held businesses in the commercial and financial services industries. Julie is a certified public accountant, and is a member of the American Accounting Association and The American Institute of Certified Public Accountants.

In addition to teaching, Julie serves on the finance committee for the United Way of Champaign County and is Director of the Accountancy Internship Program at the University of Illinois at Urbana-Champaign.

Cynthia W. Turner is a lecturer in accountancy at the University of Illinois in Urbana-Champaign. A summa cum laude graduate of North Carolina A&T State University, Cynthia received her MA and PhD from The Ohio State University. For the past 16 years, Cynthia has taught courses in managerial accounting and auditing on both the undergraduate and graduate levels. As a member of the first faculty group to implement Project Discovery (an active learning curriculum) at the University of Illinois, Cynthia has used case instruction and the team-based learning approach throughout her teaching career. Cynthia has received several student awards for outstanding teaching and has been consistently listed on the University of Illinois's "Incomplete List of Teachers Ranked as Excellent."

Cynthia's scholarly work has been published in the *Journal of Accounting Research* and the *International Journal of Accounting*, and prior to beginning her academic career, Cynthia was a practicing accountant at Ernst & Young, LLP. Cynthia is a certified public accountant, and is a member of the American Accounting Association and the American Institute of Certified Public Accountants.

In addition to teaching, Cynthia is Associate Director of the Undergraduate Accountancy Program at the University of Illinois at Urbana-Champaign. Further, she works extensively throughout her community serving as a board member and consultant to several local organizations and as a mentor and advisor to a number of student groups.

Acknowledgments

We would like to thank our families for their wonderful support while we were engaged in writing this case book. We would also like to thank Dr. Gene King and Mr. Sanford Hess for the rich wealth of information they generously shared with us regarding their daily business operations.

We are grateful to Ginny Munroe, Stephanie Wall, and Nicole Sam for their editorial support. We are especially appreciative of the insightful comments and helpful suggestions offered by our peer reviewers. Finally, we express our sincere gratitude for the exceptional work of our research assistants, particularly Carol Sung.

Reviewers

We would like to thank the following reviewers for their insightful comments and contributions to the development of these cases.

Patricia Worsham	*Riverside Community College*
Janet O'Tousa	*University of Notre Dame*
Michael J. Meyer	*University of Notre Dame*
Jean Riley-Schultz	*University of Nebraska - Lincoln*
Catherine Jeppson	*California State University - Northridge*
Mitchell Franklin	*Syracuse University*
Freda McBride	*Elizabeth City State University*
Thomas Kam	*Hawaii Pacific University*
Marci Butterfield	*University of Utah*
Sheila Ammons	*Austin Community College*
Lawrence Chui	*University of St. Thomas*

Julia Shapland and Cynthia Turner

Project DJ

Ted Miller

1 Project DJ

1 Project DJ

Ted Miller was born and raised in Baltimore, MD where he spent most of his youth involved in music. From playing the trumpet in his school jazz band to playing the drums in a neighborhood rock band, Ted was always performing on some musical stage. At the age of 18, while a freshman at the University of Maryland-Baltimore, Ted recalls going to a campus party where he heard an especially talented DJ scratch and mix beats together in such a way that he worked the crowd to a fever pitch. It was in that moment that Ted knew he wanted to do the same thing. Within 6 months, he purchased some used DJ turntables and some vinyl records. Also a charmer, Ted was able to bribe his mom into buying him headphones, and soon began practicing everyday after class. By the following fall, Ted found himself back at the same venue, but this time *he* was in the DJ booth.

Throughout his college years, Ted (aka "DJ Teddy") gained popularity on campus and before long was playing for a packed house nearly 5 days a week. Whether it was in the basement of a fraternity house or in an uptown nightclub, his services were in great demand and, as a consequence, he was able to hone his DJ skills while at the same time pay for his music production degree. During his senior year, Ted began to distribute demo tapes to anyone who would listen. One of the tapes reached the hands of a fellow student whose uncle owned many of Baltimore's most popular nightclubs. Soon thereafter, Ted was hired as the lead DJ at one of the biggest nightclubs in Baltimore—The Metro.

After graduating from college, Ted began working at The Metro 6 days a week. Within two years, he won the *Baltimore Post's* prestigious "beat" award after its readers voted him the best nightclub DJ in the city. Winning this award had always been a dream of his, and the local recognition served him well. His services were in such high demand, he could literally name his own price. However, after 15 years of playing the club circuit, Ted was ready for a change.

This course project was prepared by Julia P. Shapland and Cynthia W. Turner of the University of Illinois at Urbana-Champaign for classroom use and discussion. All businesses and characters appearing in this work are fictitious. Any resemblance to existing businesses or real persons, living or dead, is purely coincidental.

The change came in late October of 2008 when Ted heard that the successful, local business Music Express (ME) was closing its doors. Owners Joe and Donna Lowry had started Music Express 24 years earlier, and it was considered by many to be one of the community's premier music providers. Music Express provided DJ services at hundreds of events per year and maintained a loyal customer base in the metro area. Despite Music Express's success, Joe and Donna had begun to find Baltimore's harsh winters unbearable and wished to move to a warmer climate. With no other choices available to them, the Lowrys planned to auction off the assets and simply close ME's doors forever.

For quite a while, Ted had been pondering the idea of leaving the nightclub scene in order to exclusively service private parties and weddings. He had grown tired of working 5-6 nights per week, and more importantly, he no longer wanted to work for someone else. The idea of serving a different sector of the community appealed to him, as did the ability to be selective of the parties at which he played. Further, since getting into the business, he had witnessed a significant increase in the popularity of nightclub DJs working private parties (especially weddings). The modern wedding couple now wanted their reception to have the look of elegance and the feel of a party; and they were willing to spend premium dollars for this experience. This, in turn, meant well-known DJs could often pick and choose at what events they would play and live quite comfortably off only a few events per month, leaving plenty of time for other interests.

When Ted contacted the Lowrys, they relished the idea that their brainchild Music Express would continue to exist and provide music to the Baltimore community for years to come. Negotiations moved swiftly, and in early December 2008, Ted purchased the business.

As Music Express's new owner, Ted realized that with his limited business background, he would need to learn how to make business decisions that were not based solely on a "checkbook balance." Upon meeting with his former college roommate Justin Phillips (who now owned a successful Baltimore accounting practice), Ted became convinced that maintaining accrual basis financial records for his business was the way to go. Justin pointed out that this extra effort would provide Ted with better information for decision making and would also be useful in attracting additional investors if he ever chose to expand the business. Lucky for Ted, he was able to hire Justin, who agreed to prepare Music Express's monthly, accrual basis financial statements.

Case 1-1

Analyzing Monthly Transactions

DJ Ted Miller, the new owner of Music Express (ME), has recently hired accountant Justin Phillips (his former college roommate) to assist him in setting up ME's financial records on the accrual basis as well as prepare its monthly financial statements. In order to assist him with his work, Ted has provided Justin with the following items:

- *Exhibit 1.1*: ME's Chart of Accounts.
- *Exhibit 1.2*: Ted's notes. (Although Ted did not record any transactions, he did keep detailed notes regarding the transactions and events that took place during his first few weeks of business. This exhibit represents a summary of his notes.)

Requirements:

Assume the role of accountant Justin Phillips and complete the following:

1. Using the account titles provided for you in *Exhibit 1.1* and referring back to the ***Narrative*** as needed, please prepare journal entries (using good form) *as necessary* for the transactions and events described in the accompanying exhibits for this case.[1] That is, you should prepare only those *specific* entries required to record the transactions described in these materials. You are not to consider adjusting entries that would be recorded after the events described in these exhibits.
2. Using the journal entries that you prepared in requirement (1), post the entries to "T" accounts and calculate the overall account balances as of 12/31/08.
3. Using the ending balances in the "T" accounts from requirement (2), prepare a 12/31/08 unadjusted trial balance for Music Express (ME).
4. For each account listed on the unadjusted trial balance prepared in requirement (3), identify the type of account (asset, liability, equity, revenue, or expense), and indicate whether it would be reported on the balance sheet or on the income statement. Consider also whether

[1] Before preparing your entries, take some time to review *Exhibit 1.1* and consider the nature of the accounts provided (asset, liability, equity, revenue, or expense).

any account balance is abnormal. (That is, determine whether an account balance that is expected to carry a debit balance has a credit balance and vice versa.) If you determine that a particular account balance is abnormal, label it as such and explain what the abnormal balance communicates.

5. Using your unadjusted account balances from requirement (3), calculate the following items as of 12/31/08:

    a. Total dollar amount of ME's assets.

    b. Total dollar amount of ME's liabilities.

    c. Total equity (using the balance sheet equation).

    d. The unadjusted net income (or net loss).

    (In order to earn credit, you must provide the name and dollar amount of the underlying accounts that make up your answer.)

6. Using the balance you computed for total equity in requirement 5(c), determine how much of this balance is

    a. Total contributed capital.

    b. Total retained earnings.

7. As of 12/31/08, how much money is owed to ME by its customers? On which financial statement would this balance be reported?

8. Consider each of the liabilities identified in requirement 5(b) and comment on how the liability will eventually be settled.

9. Consider the holiday gift that Ted treated himself to on 12/23 (*Exhibit 1.2*). Using the accounts listed in *Exhibit 1.1*, provide at least two possible alternatives for the debit portion of the resulting journal entry and explain how the economic entity assumption impacts your choices. Given your two options, please clarify what additional information you would need from Ted in order to determine which specific classification best captures the economic reality of this situation.

Case 1-2

Recording Month-End Adjustments

To date, accountant Justin Phillips (Ted's former college roommate) has assisted Ted by recording ME's December transactions. He is now ready to prepare the December adjusting entries. In order to assist him with his work, Ted has provided Justin with the following items:

- *Exhibit 1.3*: Summary of events that took place during the first two weeks of January 2009.
- *Exhibit 1.4*: Start-up Loan Amortization Schedule.
- *Exhibit TN 1.1*: The 12/31/08 unadjusted account balances for ME ***(available from your instructor).*** *(These balances should be used as your beginning account balances.)*

Requirements:

Assume the role of accountant Justin Phillips and complete the following:

1. Determine which 12/31/08 account balances (*Exhibit TN 1.1*) require adjustment and prepare the entries.[1] Please make *all* adjustments that are necessary in order to produce proper accrual basis financial statements.[2]
2. Post the adjusting journal entries from requirement (1) to "T" accounts and calculate the overall account balances as of 12/31/08.
3. Use the ending balances in the "T" accounts from requirement (2) to prepare a 12/31/08 adjusted trial balance for ME.
4. How would the 2008 and 2009 financial statements be different if Ted had instead chosen to use the cash-basis method of accounting?
5. Which method (that is, accrual or cash-basis) provides a more meaningful and relevant picture for financial statement users? Explain using specific examples from ME to support your opinion.

---

[1] Please use the account titles listed in *Exhibit TN 1.1* for purposes of your entries. If you need to create a new account, please do so, but clearly label it as to its type (i.e., asset, liability, equity, revenue, or expense).

[2] After considering the information provided in *Exhibit 1.3*, determine whether there are any *additional* adjustments that need to be made in order to produce proper accrual basis financial statements. Start by going through the unadjusted trial balance in *Exhibit TN 1.1* and for each account balance ask yourself, "Is this a deferred revenue or expense?" If so, then determine whether the account balance requires adjustment as of 12/31/08. For each of the remaining accounts, then ask yourself, "Is there any accrued revenue or accrued expense related to this account that still needs to be recorded?

6. Please consider the 12/31/08 adjusting entries you proposed in requirement (1) related to the interest incurred on the $25,000 start-up loan and the insurance coverage for the new van. Taking into account your 12/31/08 adjustments for these two items, propose the entries that would be recorded by ME in January of 2009 at the time of the cash payments (*Exhibit 1.3*, (i) and (iv)).

Case 1-3

Preparing the Financial Statements

Since being hired as ME's accountant, Justin Phillips (Ted's former college roommate) has recorded the December transactions and adjusting entries. He is now ready to prepare ME's 12/31/08 financial statements and has been provided the following item:

- *Exhibit TN 1.2*: The final 12/31/2008 account balances after all adjusting entries ***(available from your instructor)***.

Requirements:

Assume the role of accountant Justin Phillips and complete the following:

1. Using good form, prepare the following December 31, 2008 financial statements:[1]
   a. The Balance Sheet.
   b. The Income Statement.
   c. The Statement of Shareholder's Equity.
2. Prepare all necessary closing entries.
3. Prepare a post-closing trial balance *(in good form)*.
4. Please answer the questions below.
   a. Why are closing entries necessary?
   b. Why should the income summary account never appear on a financial statement?

[1] In order to determine the proper classification of the account balances included in *Exhibit TN 1.2*, you are encouraged to review the ***Narrative*** and, if necessary, information provided in *Exhibits 1.1-1.4*.

Exhibit 1.1: Chart of Accounts*

Accounts Payable
Accounts Receivable
Accumulated Depreciation
Advertising Expense
Amortization Expense
Cash
Common Stock
Customer Deposits
Depreciation Expense
Dividend Income
Dividend paid to owner
Due from owner
Due to owner
Insurance Expense
Insurance Payable
Interest Expense
Interest Payable
Interest Receivable
Interest Revenue
Long-Term Investments
Miscellaneous Expense
Music Equipment
Music Expense
Music Library
Note Payable
Office Equipment
Other Receivable
Prepaid Advertising
Prepaid Insurance
Prepaid Interest
Prepaid Rent
Professional Fees
Rent Expense
Rent Payable
Repair & Maintenance
Retained Earnings
Salaries Expense
Salaries Payable
Service Fees Earned
Supplies
Supplies Expense
Training & Development Expense
Travel Expense
Utilities Expense
Utilities Payable
Vehicles

*If you need to create a new account, please do so, but clearly label it as to its type (asset, liability, equity, revenue, or expense).

Exhibit 1.2: Ted's Notes[1]

Saturday, November 15:

Ted met with his banker and received pre-approval for a $25,000 business start-up loan.

Sunday, November 30:

Ted met with his attorney and filed the necessary paperwork to create a corporation called Music Express, Inc. ("ME").

Monday, December 1:

i. Ted deposited $35,000 of his personal savings into the newly opened business checking account, and in exchange, he received 100% of the corporate stock.
ii. The start-up loan was finalized (with a 12/1 effective date), and $25,000 was deposited into the business checking account.
iii. ME paid the Lowrys $38,850 for the following items:

$35,000	for used music equipment
5,000	for digitized music files
4,000	for accounts receivable relating to October and November 2008 events
-2,950	less obligations to customers for advance deposits
-2,200	less amounts owed for November rent
$38,850	

Friday, December 5:

i. ME paid the local radio station $4,500, and in return, received 90 days of radio advertising. The advertising spots will begin on 12/15 and run on a daily basis through 3/14/2009.
ii. ME got off to a great start by performing at a local Chamber of Commerce holiday function. Before leaving the event, Ted collected a check for $600.

Saturday, December 6:

i. Ted mailed a bill for the balance owed for the 12/5 Chamber of Commerce event.

Total charges for event	$1,500
Less: credit for deposit already made	-200
Less: payment made on the day of event	-600
Balance due	$ 700

[1] The dates provided in this exhibit are for 2008.

ii. Ted hired a local painter to freshen up the look of the reception area. The painter gave him a great deal, quoting $500 for the entire job. Work will begin 12/8 and should be finished by 12/10.

iii. ME provided the music at two smaller events sponsored by student groups at the University.

Sunday, December 7:

Ted served as DJ at an afternoon event at a local church. Before leaving, he collected $300.

Monday, December 8:

i. Ted mailed bills for the 12/6 and 12/7 events:

	12/6	12/7	Total
Total charges for event	$1,900	$700	$2,600
Less: credit for deposit already made	-400	-0	-400
Less: payment made on the day of the event	-0	-300	-300
Balance due	$1,500	$400	$1,900

ii. Ted met with an insurance agent and paid $2,730 total for the following two policies: (a) a $1,200 12-month liability policy effective 12/1, and (b) a $1,530 18-month property insurance policy also effective 12/1.

iii. Paid $2,200 for the November rent.

Tuesday, December 9:

i. Paid $300 to the local newspapers for an employment ad which ran on 12/7 in the weekend job finder supplement.

ii. The mail contained $2,800 of customer payments. $1,500 represented payments for events held in October and November of 2008, and $1,300 represented deposits toward events to be held in 2009.

Wednesday, December 10:

i. Received a $1,300 bill from the attorney for his December services.

ii. Received a utility bill in the mail totaling $750! The bill was for October and November utilities plus late fees. Concerned that his utilities would be shut off, Ted paid the bill. Ted then called his attorney who confirmed that he (the attorney) had overlooked these items when negotiating with the Lowrys. His attorney immediately sent a letter to the Lowrys requesting they reimburse Ted for this payment.

Thursday, December 11:

i. Ted paid $600 to Ripped Music Company for use of its current music demos to record various music sets.

ii. Ted received a good response to his employment ad, and as a result, he interviewed three potential candidates. He ultimately signed employment contracts with two part-time employees. The employees will start work on 12/22, and are anticipated to work between 15 and 20 hours per week. Both individuals had experience in the entertainment industry and were willing to come in the week before they started for a quick training session on the equipment. Ted plans to pay his employees every other Friday with their first pay-period beginning Friday, January 2.

Friday, December 12:

i. Ted was enthused when a bride and her mother unexpectedly stopped in to discuss the music for an upcoming July 2009 wedding. Even though they were not aware that ME was under new ownership, they knew of Ted and were excited to find out that he would be the DJ. Before leaving, they made a $600 deposit to lock in the date. Ted quoted them a price of $2,100 to provide 5 hours of music at the wedding reception.
ii. The mail contained $1,400 of customer payments relating to events held in October and November 2008.

Saturday, December 13:

ME provided the music at a local charity function.

Monday, December 15:

i. Ted mailed a bill for the 12/13 event detailing the following amount due:

Total charges for event	$700
Less: credit for deposit already made	-0
Balance due	$700

ii. Paid the painter $650. (The painter ended up using more paint and, as a result, charged Ted more than his original quote.)
iii. Ted purchased $800 of office supplies (including custom stationery and business cards) on account.

Tuesday, December 16:

Ted received the balance due from the church gig on 12/7.

Monday, December 22:

With the holiday season well underway, this week was very busy. Between the three employees, ME had worked 9 separate holiday events! Ted still could not believe that he had earned $14,000 in just one week. Most of the event organizers had paid him in cash on the day of the event, but for those events where he had not yet been paid, Ted was sure to email a bill before leaving the venue.

Bills emailed by Ted:	
Total charges for events	$14,000
Less: credit for deposits already made	-1,200
Less: payments made on the day of the events	-9,000
Balance due	$ 3,800

Tuesday, December 23:

Ted treated himself to a holiday gift and paid $2,500 (out of the business checking account) for reservations on a seven-day luxury cruise scheduled to occur in mid-February of 2009.

Friday, December 26:

i. Ted received a call from his banker. An $825 check received as payment from a customer on 12/12 had bounced!
ii. Ted paid the attorney his balance owed, and also paid $500 towards the supplies purchased on 12/15.
iii. Ted collected $700 of the amount owed from the 12/22 events.

Monday, December 29:

Ted purchased a Ford van (with a customized logo wrap) to be used to drive to events. The final negotiated price was $30,000. Ted wrote a check for a 25% down payment, and signed a loan with the dealership for the balance owed. He scheduled an appointment to bring the van back in January to have the logo wrap installed.

Wednesday, December 31:

Ted performed at two back-to-back New Year's Eve gigs. In each case, he emailed a bill to the event organizers before leaving the venue.

	12/31
Total charges for two events	$6,500
Less: credit for deposits already made	-500
Less: payments made on the day of the event	-3,000
Balance due	$3,000

Exhibit 1.3: Summary of January 2009 Events

Thursday, January 1:

i. Ted made his first $477.53 loan payment on the $25,000 start-up loan (*Exhibit 1.2*, 12/1(ii); *Exhibit 1.4*). As he wrote the check, Ted gave a sigh of relief that his auto loan for his new van had no payment due until March and charged zero interest!

ii. Ted counted the office supplies noting that after the frenzy of holiday parties, they only had $200 of supplies remaining.

iii. Ted ordered $400 of supplies and paid the balance due for the supplies purchased back in December (*Exhibit 1.2*, 12/15(iii) and 12/26(ii)).

iv. Ted dropped off a $350 check at his insurance agent's office. The payment was for the auto insurance on the new van (*Exhibit 1.2*, 12/29). He had called last week and arranged for the coverage (180 days, effective at 12:01 a.m. on the date of purchase).

Friday, January 2:

i. Ted wrote payroll checks to his employees totaling $2,760. Payroll was calculated based on the hours submitted by the employees in their weekly time sheets (as detailed in Figure 1.1). Ted could not be happier with the competence and professionalism of his new hires; and even though he is paying them $30 per hour, he feels like he is the one getting the "good deal!"

Figure 1.1

	Employee #1 Hours	Employee #2 Hours
22-Dec	9	10
23-Dec	7	9
24-Dec	2	1
26-Dec	1	2
27-Dec	5	7
29-Dec	4	-
31-Dec	8	9
1-Jan	4	3
2-Jan	5	6
	45	47

ii. As Ted prepared the payroll and reviewed time sheets, he was surprised to discover that he had not billed for the New Year's Eve and New Year's Day parties worked by his two employees! Thankful for the catch, he prepared and mailed invoices for these events as indicated in Figure 1.2.

Figure 1.2

	Employee 1	Employee 2	Total
Total charges for events	$3,600	$1,800	$5,400
Less: credit for deposits already made	-400	-250	-650
Amount owed	3,200	1,550	4,750
Less: payments made on the day of the event	-1,400	- 0	-1,400
Balance due for New Year's Eve parties	$1,800	$1,550	$3,350

	Employee 1	Employee 2	Total
Total charges for events	$625	$1,100	$1,725
Less: credit for deposits already made	-0	-200	-200
Amount owed	625	900	1,525
Less: payments made on the day of the event	-0	-400	-400
Balance due for New Year's Day parties	$625	$500	$1,125
Grand Total	$2,425	$2,050	$4,475

Saturday, January 3:

Federal Express delivered an HP laser jet printer that Ted ordered during the last week in December. Given a regular cost of $265, Ted was excited to buy it online for only $225 dollars! However, he had overlooked the shipping charges and was disappointed when he noticed the additional $50 charge for shipping (the printer was shipped FOB shipping point on 12/29).

Monday, January 5:

i. Ted opened the mail and found the following items:

   a. Customer payments totaling $5,650. $900 of this represented advance deposits for 2009 events and $4,750 represented payments from customers on account ($2,250 for outstanding balances relating to December events and $2,500 relating to October/November events).
   b. The December utility bill totaling $525.
   c. The December phone bill totaling $250 (this amount included $125 of extra charges for installation and new account fees).
   d. A $750 check from the Lowrys for the October and November utilities (*Exhibit 1.2*, 12/10(ii)).

Tuesday, January 6:

Ted deposited $5,750 of the cash received on the prior day (Monday, January 5) and kept $650 to spend personally. He wrote and mailed checks paying the December rent ($2,200) and the December utilities and phone bill.

Thursday, January 8:

i. After discussions with his accountant Justin, Ted decided to use straight-line depreciation for all assets except the vehicles (which he will depreciate using units-of-production). Justin provided him with the following summary:

Asset	Useful Life
Music Equipment	36 months
Music Library	24 months[2]
Vehicle	60,000 miles

While Ted had only owned the new van for 10 days, he had already put over 1,000 miles on it! In fact, he only owned the van for 2 days in 2008, but still managed to accumulate 225 miles!

ii. Before leaving Justin's office, Ted paid him $125 for his professional time.

iii. Ted has not yet obtained a corporate credit card and has been charging any fuel purchases to his personal credit card. Following Justin's recommendation, Ted went back through his receipts and reimbursed himself (via the business checking account) for the business-related fuel purchases.

December 2008:	$ 35
January 2009:	$135
Total gas purchases	$170

Friday, January 9:

Ted took his new van back to the dealership and had the logo wrap installed. He paid $1,100 of the charges before leaving the facility.

[2] The music library is considered an intangible asset and would be amortized using straight-line over its useful life. For purposes of calculating amortization on the new music sets purchased on 12/11 (*Exhibit 1.2*), assume that ME takes one-half a month of amortization in the first and last month of the asset's life.

Exhibit 1.4: Start-up Loan Amortization Schedule

(prepared by bank)

Payment Date	Payment	Interest	Principal	Balance
				$25,000.00
1/1/2009	$477.53	114.58	(362.95)	$24,637.05
2/1/2009	$477.53	112.92	(364.61)	$24,272.44
3/1/2009	$477.53	111.25	(366.28)	$23,906.16
4/1/2009	$477.53	109.57	(367.96)	$23,538.20
5/1/2009	$477.53	107.88	(369.65)	$23,168.56
6/1/2009	$477.53	106.19	(371.34)	$22,797.21
7/1/2009	$477.53	104.49	(373.04)	$22,424.17
8/1/2009	$477.53	102.78	(374.75)	$22,049.42
9/1/2009	$477.53	101.06	(376.47)	$21,672.95
10/1/2009	$477.53	99.33	(378.20)	$21,294.75
11/1/2009	$477.53	97.60	(379.93)	$20,914.82
12/1/2009	$477.53	95.86	(381.67)	$20,533.15
1/1/2010	$477.53	94.11	(383.42)	$20,149.73
2/1/2010	$477.53	92.35	(385.18)	$19,764.56
3/1/2010	$477.53	90.59	(386.94)	$19,377.61

Julia Shapland and Cynthia Turner

Project Wedding Planner

Ellen Litchfield

2 Project Wedding Planner

2 Project Wedding Planner

About 30 years ago after the birth of her second child, lawyer Ellen Litchfield decided to abandon her thriving legal career to become a stay-at-home mother. As with all her endeavors, Ellen threw herself fully into the parenting process, and together with her husband Dave, they raised five beautiful daughters. Consequently, when Ellen's youngest daughter Samantha married, Ellen and Dave found themselves for the first time facing an empty nest. Nonetheless, this significant transition came with quite a send-off in the form of Samantha's wedding. Ellen spent 14 months planning this monumental event, and much to her surprise, her hard work did not go unnoticed. In fact, her daughter's wedding became the talk of the town and many of her friends began to ask her to plan their children's weddings. After several years of planning weddings for her family and friends, Ellen's reputation spread throughout the community. Requests for her paid services soon followed, and she recognized the need to formally set up her own business. On June 1, 2009, An Affair 2 Remember (AA2R) officially opened its first retail space, located in a newly renovated historic building in the downtown district.

The Business of AA2R

AA2R plans everything from small, private gatherings to large, formal affairs. No matter the size of the occasion, Ellen has a reputation for paying attention to even the smallest detail. She has a wide variety of quality vendors at her disposal, and she always knows just who to call to find that special but hard-to-find item. Ellen's consulting fees range from $1,500 (minimal services) to as high as $25,000. She collects her consulting fees upfront and varies them based on the size and complexity of the event. In addition, she contracts for all wedding-related services (photographer, flowers, music, food, and so on) and receives the invoices for the services rendered. Once she verifies the accuracy of each invoice, she pays them and then bills her

---

This course project was prepared by Julia P. Shapland and Cynthia W. Turner of the University of Illinois at Urbana-Champaign for classroom use and discussion. All businesses and characters appearing in this work are fictitious. Any resemblance to existing businesses or real persons, living or dead, is purely coincidental.

customer for reimbursement plus a moderate handling fee. Most payments are made with a check, however, Ellen also uses the debit card associated with the business checking account for certain online purchases.

Because wedding costs can be sizable, Ellen is careful to bill frequently and keep a close eye on customer collections. So far, most couples have been good about paying on a timely basis. However, Ellen recognizes nonpayment as a significant risk factor in her current business model.

Ellen provides all prospective clients with an initial, one-hour consultation, free of charge. After the initial consultation, Ellen provides the couple with a contract, detailing the terms of her services. Upon receiving the signed contract, Ellen gets right to work by holding a series of planning meetings. In most cases, the couple arrives at the first meeting with a very clear vision of their special day, but with no real understanding of the true cost of their "dream wedding." Even though Ellen is a master at creating beautiful events on small budgets, she knows that it is critical for the couple to establish realistic expectations about their wedding day and what type of event they can truly afford. Therefore, one of her first priorities is to establish a wedding budget and help the couple to decide how the budget will be spent. This process can be difficult and emotional with each person needing to sacrifice part of their "dream." Ellen is gifted at facilitating this process and often feels that she is part marriage counselor and part wedding planner. In most cases, both the bride and groom finish the negotiations pleased with the outcome. Once she has an approved budget, Ellen gets right to work planning the event while trying to squeeze as much out of each dollar as possible. Ellen keeps careful records of her spending and continues to meet frequently with the couple so that they are aware of the costs being incurred. She lets the couple know immediately if any of their selections place them over budget (although in her experience, it is rare for couples to stay within their initial budget).

Upon starting the business, Ellen negotiated an open line of credit agreement with her local bank. In order to keep tabs on the health of the business, the loan officer has required that, starting with the quarter ending June 30, 2009, she provide him with quarterly, accrual basis financial statements.

Case 2-1

Analyzing Monthly Transactions

Ellen Litchfield recently shared with your accounting professor (who happens to be a friend) the news of her latest start-up venture, An Affair 2 Remember (AA2R). In her discussion with your professor, Ellen mentions that, starting with the quarter ending June 30, 2009, she is required to provide her bank loan officer with quarterly, accrual basis financial statements. Ellen further explains that, although she enjoys keeping the checkbook and paying the bills, she really has no idea about how to prepare a set of financial statements. Seeing this task as a great course assignment, your professor offers to have your class help, beginning with recording monthly transaction activity.

Ellen provides your class with the following materials to assist you with your work:

- *Exhibit 2.1*: AA2R's Chart of Accounts.
- *Exhibit 2.2*: Although Ellen did not record any transactions, she did keep detailed notes regarding the transactions and events that took place during her first two months of business. This exhibit represents a summary of her notes.
- *Exhibit 2.3 a-e*: Client billing statements.

Requirements:

1. Using the account titles provided for you in *Exhibit 2.1* and referring back to the ***Narrative*** as needed, please prepare journal entries (using good form) *as necessary* for the transactions and events described in the accompanying exhibits for this case.[1] That is, you should prepare only those *specific* entries required to record the transactions described in these materials. You are not to consider adjusting entries that would be recorded after the events described in these exhibits.
2. Using the journal entries that you prepared in requirement (1), post the entries to "T" accounts and calculate the overall account balances as of 6/30/09.

---

[1] Before preparing your entries, take some time to review *Exhibit 2.1* and consider the nature of the accounts provided (asset, liability, equity, revenue, or expense).

3. Using the ending balances in the "T" accounts from requirement (2), prepare a 6/30/09 unadjusted trial balance for AA2R.

4. For each account listed on the unadjusted trial balance prepared in requirement (3), identify the type of account (asset, liability, equity, revenue, or expense), and indicate whether it would be reported on the balance sheet or the income statement. Consider also whether any account balance is abnormal. (That is, determine whether an account balance that is expected to carry a debit balance has a credit balance and vice versa.) If you determine that a particular account balance is abnormal, label it as such and explain what the abnormal balance communicates.

5. Using your unadjusted account balances from requirement (3), calculate the following items as of 6/30/2009:

   a. Total dollar amount of AA2R's assets.

   b. Total dollar amount of AA2R's liabilities.

   c. Total equity (using the balance sheet equation).

   d. The unadjusted net income (or net loss).

   (In order to earn credit, you must provide the name and dollar amount of the underlying accounts that make up your answer.)

6. Using the balance you computed for total equity in requirement 5(c), determine how much of this balance is

   a. Total contributed capital.

   b. Total retained earnings.

7. Consider each of the liabilities identified in requirement 5(b) and comment on how the liability will eventually be settled.

8. Consider the champagne that Ellen and her friends consumed on June 12 (iii). Using the accounts listed in *Exhibit 2.1*, provide at least two possible alternatives for the debit portion of the resulting journal entry and explain how the economic entity assumption impacts your choices. Given your two options, please clarify what additional information you would need

from Ellen in order to determine which specific classification best captures the economic reality of this situation.

9. Please discuss the risk(s) associated with Ellen's customer accounts receivable balances and suggest changes to her business model that could reduce the risk(s).

Case 2-2

Recording Month-End Adjustments

Your accounting professor recently agreed to have your class assist entrepreneur Ellen Litchfield with the preparation of her June 30, 2009 financial statements for her new wedding planning business, An Affair 2 Remember (AA2R). To date, you have assisted Ellen by recording AA2R's June transactions, and are now ready to prepare the June adjusting entries. Your professor provides the following items to assist you in preparing the 6/30 adjustments.

- *Exhibit 2.4*: Summary of events that took place during the first two weeks of July 2009.
- *Exhibit 2.5a-c*: Client billing statements.
- *Exhibit TN 2.1*: The 6/30/09 unadjusted account balances for AA2R ***(available from your instructor)***. *(These balances should be used as your beginning account balances.)*
- *Exhibit TN 2.2*: This exhibit will be made available by the instructor to students who are ***not*** completing ***Case 2-3***. See footnote 3 (on the next page) for more details.

Requirements:

Your professor asks that you make *all* adjustments that are necessary to produce proper accrual basis financial statements as of June 30, 2009.[1] Specifically, you are to complete the following.

1. Determine which 6/30 account balances (*Exhibit TN 2.1*) require adjustment and prepare the required adjusting journal entries.[2]
2. Post the adjusting journal entries from requirement (1) to "T" accounts and calculate the overall account balances as of 6/30/09.
3. Use the ending balances in the "T" accounts from requirement (2) to prepare a 06/30/09 adjusted trial balance for AA2R.[3]

[1] After considering the information provided in *Exhibit 2.4*, determine whether there are any *additional* adjustments that need to be made in order to produce proper accrual basis financial statements. Start by going through the unadjusted trial balance in *Exhibit TN 2.1* and for each account balance ask yourself, "Is this a deferred revenue or expense?" If so, then determine whether the account balance requires adjustment as of 6/30/09. For each of the remaining accounts, then ask yourself, "Is there any accrued revenue or accrued expense related to this account that still needs to be recorded?

[2] Please use the account titles listed in *Exhibit TN 2.1* for purposes of your entries. If you need to create a new account, please do so, but clearly label it as to its type (asset, liability, equity, revenue, or expense).

4. For each adjusting journal entry prepared in requirement (1), classify the adjustment as one of the following:
   - accrued revenue
   - accrued expense
   - adjustment of an existing deferred revenue
   - adjustment of an existing deferred expense
   - error correction[4]

5. Prepare a listing of the individual customers and their corresponding balances that make up the ending Accounts Receivable balance.

6. Briefly describe the "Unearned Consultation Fees" account. Explain how and why it is used. How is this account different than the "Wedding Consultation Fees Earned" account? Explain the term "earned" and how the revenue recognition criteria influence the need to have both of these accounts.

---

[3] If you are required to complete ***Case 2-3***, you will prepare additional adjusting entries as a result of the information provided in that case, and your adjusted trial balance will accordingly not be finalized until after these additional entries. If you are not required to complete ***Case 2-3*** you should receive *Exhibit TN 2.2* from your instructor which will provide you with the necessary information to prepare all adjusting entries as well as your final adjusted trial balance.

[4] An error does not necessarily only include something that was initially recorded improperly, but could include something that should have been recorded in June that was not.

Case 2-3

Preparing the Bank Reconciliation

Your professor recently met Ellen for lunch to discuss what additional items your class would need in order to assist her in finalizing the June financial statements for her company. Over the last few weeks, your class has assisted Ellen in recording AA2R's June transactions and most of its adjusting entries. Your class is now ready to finalize the June adjustments by recording those that result from the June bank reconciliation.

During their lunch meeting, Ellen mentions to your professor that although her assistant Sherri could prepare the bank reconciliation, she was hoping instead that this task could be assigned to your class as part of the financial statement project. Ellen privately shares that, just recently, she discovered Sherri had stolen champagne from AA2R. As a result, she is legitimately concerned about Sherri's trustworthiness and longevity as an employee. Upon hearing this, your professor readily agrees to have your class take on this additional task.

Ellen, who is always quite diplomatic, adds that other than the "champagne situation," Sherri is doing a great job. Specifically, Ellen shares that Sherri single-handedly planned and coordinated a highly successful "meet & greet," which led to some new clients. She also notes that Sherri provided a great recommendation for a photographer/videographer when she suggested her cousin Dave, who runs a professional photography studio (Bolder Image) out of his home. So far, Ellen has been pleased with the quality of the work Dave has provided and is extremely appreciative to Sherri for making the referral.

At your professor's invitation, Ellen stops by your class and discusses the accounting system surrounding AA2R's customer receipts and vendor disbursements. She also provides the following documentation to assist you with your preparation of the June bank reconciliation.

- Exhibit 2.6a: The June bank statement received in the mail in early July (prepared by the bank).
- Exhibit 2.6b: Details of items noted in the June bank statement.

- *Exhibit 2.7*: Ellen's summary schedules.[1]
- *Exhibit TN 2.3*: A photocopy of AA2R's checkbook ***(available from your instructor)***.
- *Exhibit TN 2.4*: Details of the general ledger cash balance reported in *Exhibit TN 2.5* (needed for requirement (2) only— ***available from your instructor***).
- *Exhibit TN 2.5*: The 6/30/2009 account balances that include all necessary adjusting entries *except* those additional entries that will be recorded in this case ***(available from your instructor)***.

AA2R's Accounting System

Customer Receipts: Most customers send in their remittance by mail, although they may occasionally drop the payment off in person. If Ellen is out of the office (as she is quite frequently), her assistant Sherri is responsible for opening the mail. If a client payment is included, Sherri will stamp it with a restrictive endorsement, make a photo copy (to put in the client file), and prepare the deposit ticket. Ellen (or possibly Sherri) then drops the deposit off in the night depository at the bank.

Cash Disbursements: When vendor invoices are received, Ellen (or Sherri) pulls the client file and compares the invoice to the record of services provided. Assuming they agree, a check is prepared and Ellen's summary schedule is updated (*Exhibit 2.7*).

Requirements:

1. Prepare the June bank reconciliation, reconciling the checkbook provided in *Exhibit TN 2.3* to the bank statement provided in *Exhibit 2.6a*. A reconciliation template has been provided for your use on the subsequent pages. Be sure to clearly explain all reconciling items.
2. Please complete the following:
    a. Compare the final reconciled checkbook balance (that is, the final answer from requirement (1)) to the cash balance reported on the general ledger (*Exhibits TN 2.4* and *2.5*), and explain all differences noted (if any).

[1] If you encounter a discrepancy between the checkbook and the bank statement, please note that the numbers reported in this exhibit (prepared by Ellen) are correct and do not contain errors. That is, the cost summaries provided in *Exhibit 2.7* accurately represent (i) all wedding costs incurred to date, and (ii) all vendor payments made (and authorized by Ellen) during the month of June.

b. Prepare all adjusting entries that are necessary as a result of the bank reconciliation process.[2]

c. Consider whether there is anything else that should be brought to Ellen's attention as a result of your findings from reconciling the cash account. If so, explain.

3. When LLSM Finance withdrew the first auto loan payment directly from Ellen's checking account, the bank reported this as a "debit" entry on the bank statement. You are likely familiar with a "debit card," which allows you to immediately withdraw cash from your personal bank account. We have learned in class that a positive cash balance is an asset, and that an asset's balance decreases with a credit entry and increases with a debit entry. If this is the case, why do banks refer to such withdrawals (account reductions) as "debits?" Please explain.

[2] Please provide a thorough description of all proposed entries and use the account titles listed in *Exhibit TN 2.5* for purposes of your entries. If you need to create a new account, please do so, but clearly label it as to its type (asset, liability, equity, revenue, or expense).

Bank Balance per 6/30 Bank Statement $ 17,719.80

Plus: Deposits in Transit (list individually)

Errors and other items (list individually and explain):

Explanation

Less: Outstanding Checks (list individually)

Errors and other items (list individually and explain):

Explanation

Reconciled Balance per Bank at 6/30 $

Unadjusted Balance per Checkbook at 6/30 $ (3,289.20)

Plus: Interest earned during June ______________

Errors and other items (list individually and explain):

Explanation

______________ ______________

______________ ______________

______________ ______________

______________ ______________

Less: Bank Service Fee ______________

Errors and other items (list individually and explain):

Explanation

______________ ______________

______________ ______________

______________ ______________

______________ ______________

Reconciled Balance per Checkbook at 6/30 $______________

Case 2-4

Preparing the Financial Statements

You are nearing the end of your comprehensive class project for local entrepreneur and wedding planner, Ellen Litchfield. At this point in your course assignment, your class has analyzed and recorded the June, 2009 transactions, and prepared and posted journal entries and adjustments. You are now ready to complete your final task and prepare AA2R's June 30, 2009 financial statements. Ellen has provided you with the following item in order to assist you with this task.

- *Exhibit TN 2.6*: The final 6/30/2009 account balances after all adjusting entries ***(available from your instructor)***.

Requirements:

1. Using good form, prepare the following June 30, 2009 financial statements:[1]
    a. The Balance Sheet.
    b. The Income Statement.
    c. The Statement of Shareholder's Equity.[2]
2. Prepare all necessary closing entries.
3. Prepare a post-closing trial balance *(in good form)*.

[1] In order to determine the proper classification of the account balances included in *Exhibit TN 2.6*, you are encouraged to review the ***Narrative*** and, if necessary, information provided in *Exhibits 2.1-2.7*.
[2] Please note that Ellen has not made any additional capital contributions during the year.

Exhibit 2.1: Chart of Accounts*

Accounts Payable
Accounts Receivable
Accumulated Depreciation
Advertising Expense
Capital Stock
Cash
Contract Services**
Depreciation Expense
Dividend Income
Dividends Paid
Employee Receivable
Furniture & Fixtures
Insurance Expense
Interest Expense
Interest Payable
Interest Revenue
Miscellaneous Expense
Note Payable
Office Equipment
Office Furniture
Office Supplies
Office Supplies Expense
Other Miscellaneous Receivable
Prepaid Advertising
Prepaid Insurance
Prepaid Rent
Professional Fees
Promotional Expense
Promotional Supplies
Rent Expense
Repairs and Maintenance Expense
Retained Earnings
Salaries Expense
Salaries Payable
Shareholder Receivable
Shipping Expense
Training & Development Expense
Travel & Lodging Expense
Unearned Consultation Fees
Utilities Expense
Vehicles
Wedding Consultation Fees Earned

*If you need to create a new account, please do so, but clearly label it as to its type (asset, liability, equity, revenue, or expense).

**The Contract Services account is used to record the following items:

(i) Costs incurred for all wedding-related services arranged by Ellen. As explained in the ***Narrative***, these costs would include such items as the photographer, flowers, music, reception food, drinks, plus much more. As also mentioned in the ***Narrative***, Ellen pays these charges directly to the vendor and then seeks reimbursement from her clients. She records her obligation to pay the vendor (accounts payable) at the time she prepares the client billing summary (*Exhibits 2.3a-e and 2.5a-c*). The offsetting debit entry is recorded to the contract services account.

(ii) Handling fees charged by Ellen. In addition to expecting 100% reimbursement for the wedding-related services mentioned in (i), Ellen charges a moderate handling fee and records the accounts receivable in full at the time she prepares the client billing summary (*Exhibits 2.3a-e and 2.5a-c*). The offsetting credit entry is recorded to the contract services account.

Because Ellen bills for her costs plus a handling fee, the ending balance in "contract services" will be an overall credit, and represents the handling fee she has earned from providing this service to her clients.

Exhibit 2.2: Ellen's Notes[1]

Friday, May 1:

i. Ellen filed the articles of incorporation with the state of Virginia, officially creating a corporate entity named AA2R, Inc.
ii. AA2R signed a lease agreement for the downtown space and committed to pay the first 6 months of rent within 10 days of taking possession on June 1.

Monday, May 11:

i. Ellen interviewed two candidates for an administrative assistant position and immediately hired the second, more experienced candidate Sherri Loveless. Ellen mentions to your professor that she hired Sherri not only for her experience and abilities, but also for her fortitude and resilience. Sherri was a real estate agent who was also a recent divorcee now caring for two young sons. Sherri was seeking a second job to supplement her dwindling real estate commissions. Ellen felt that she would be hardworking and appreciative of the job opportunity. Sherri will start work on June 1, and work Mondays through Fridays. She will be paid $800 on the second and fourth Friday of each month.[2]
ii. Ellen made a bulk purchase of letterhead and business cards with the new corporate name and logo. The list price per the vendor catalog was $1,200. Due to the large quantity of the order, Ellen was able to negotiate a 5% trade discount off the list price. At the time the order was placed, the vendor guaranteed shipment by May 26, with shipping terms of FOB Destination.
iii. Ellen ordered custom upholstered furniture and coordinating window treatments for the new office space totaling $16,000. The furniture will be shipped (FOB destination) before the end of May and is expected to arrive before the start of business.

Friday, May 15:

AA2R applied for a $200,000 operating line of credit with American Bank (Ellen and Dave personally co-signed). This line of credit will serve as overdraft protection and will be available to cover the lag time between the incurrence of event costs and the collection of receivables.

Thursday, May 21:

AA2R received notice that the line of credit had been approved.

Wednesday, May 27:

Ellen received an email that her 5/11 bulk purchase order of supplies had been shipped.

[1] The dates provided in this exhibit are for 2009.
[2] Please ignore all payroll taxes when considering the accounting treatment of Sherri's salary.

Monday, June 1:

i. Ellen opened a checking account at American Bank in AA2R's name and legally transferred the following items to AA2R, Inc. in exchange for all of the corporate stock.
   a. Cash of $45,000.
   b. Receivable balance from Kline/Daniels May 23 Wedding: $6,500.
   c. $1,500 of office supplies.
   d. $9,500 of office equipment.

ii. Ellen dropped off a $10,800 check to her landlord representing rent from June 1 through November 30 (check #200).

iii. Ellen wrote check #201 for $2,400 to purchase the following insurance packages: a $600 Property and Casualty insurance policy effective from 6/1/09 through 5/31/10 and a $1,800 General Liability insurance policy effective from 6/1/09 through 11/30/10.

iv. Ellen purchased a new silver Ford van (with a customized logo wrap) to be used to drive to events. The final negotiated price was $28,000. At the time of purchase, Ellen wrote a check (#202) representing a 25% cash down payment and signed a note with the dealership (in AA2R's name) for the balance owed. Ellen filled in the paperwork so that the $400 monthly loan payment could be automatically withdrawn from the corporate checking account by the finance company (LLSM Finance).

v. Ellen paid $600 for auto insurance on the van (check #203). The coverage period is from 6/1/09 until 12/1/09.

vi. Sherri organized a large mailing to inform the community about AA2R. Sherri worked with local jewelers and combed the engagement announcements in the local paper to get names of newly engaged couples to invite to a promotional "meet & greet" cocktail party to be held in a few weeks.

Tuesday, June 2:

i. AA2R got off to a great start with the booking of two weddings! Although the timing was "expedited," the wedding plans were simple, and with Ellen's contacts, could be easily accomplished in the time frame requested. She collected her fee and got right to work. The details of the two events are as follows:

Contract Date	Wedding Date	Countdown[3]	Bride/Groom	Consultant Fee Collected	Initial Budget
06/02/09	06/20/09	18 days	Nickels/King	$1,500	$14,000
06/02/09	06/27/09	25 days	Braverman/Liu	$1,500	$18,000

ii. The furniture and window treatments arrived along with a bill for $17,250 (after sales tax). When Ellen's husband Dave commented on the expense of the items, Ellen explained that she plans to use the pieces for many years and she felt that it was important she make the right impression on her wealthy client base.

[3] Ellen performs the services to generate the consultant fees evenly over the wedding "count-down" period—a timeframe which ends on the wedding day.

Wednesday, June 3:

i. Ellen paid $1,500 (via debit card) for a full-page ad, which ran in the June 1 special wedding supplement published by the local paper.

ii. Ellen received her new business cards and letterhead noting payment terms of 2/10, n/30.[4]

iii. Ellen attended a Wedding Expo held in a nearby town. At the expo, she ordered 100 bottles of mid-grade champagne with a custom printed business label:

Congratulations from Ellen and the gang at AA2R!

The champagne cost $45 per bottle plus $425 for shipping. Ellen expects the champagne to be shipped FOB Shipping Point within a few days.

iv. Ellen paid $4,250 (via debit card) for 50 spots of radio advertising. The advertising spots will begin on June 15 and will run through the middle of August. The contract does not guarantee when exactly the spots will run, although the salesman showed Ellen the following distribution during his sales pitch:

- June: 15 spots
- July: 20 spots
- August: 15 spots

Thursday, June 4:

Ellen obtained a signed contract and planning fee for the Clarke/O'Neil wedding. Contract details include:

Contract Date	Wedding Date	Countdown	Consultant Fee Collected	Initial Budget
06/04/09	07/04/09	30 days	$4,800	$45,000

Friday, June 5:

Ellen received an email that the champagne ordered at the expo had been shipped.

Monday, June 8:

Sherri mailed the informational flyers as well as the invitations to the "meet & greet" scheduled for Monday, June 22. Sherri spent $625 on postage for the mass promotional mailing (check #204).

[4] For purposes of the discount, assume that the 10-day period begins at the time of title transfer.

Wednesday, June 10:

i. The champagne arrived and the labels looked great. Ellen paid the balance due in full (via debit card) after taking into account the purchase discount being offered of 1/10, n/30.[5]
ii. Ellen paid the balance due (via debit card) for the letterhead/business cards.
iii. Ellen received the $6,500 due from the Kline/Daniels wedding that took place in May. Ellen delivered the wedding album (along with a bottle of champagne) to the couple the same afternoon.

Thursday, June 11:

Ellen reviewed the invoices received for the Nickels/King and Braverman/Liu weddings and prepared billing summaries to send to each family for the wedding contract services incurred (*Exhibit 2.3a and 2.3b*). She decided to wait another few days before paying the vendor invoices.

Friday, June 12:

i. Ellen paid administrative assistant Sherri her $800 salary for the first two-week pay period (check #205).
ii. Ellen obtained a signed contract and planning fee for the Daniel/Chan wedding. Contract details include the following:

Contract Date	Wedding Date	Countdown	Consultant Fee Collected	Initial Budget
06/12/09	07/25/09	43 days	$3,500	$36,000

iii. Ellen's husband Dave and a group of her close friends stopped by with a large bouquet of roses and Thai food. Ellen uncorked a bottle of AA2R champagne, and the 10 of them, including Sherri, celebrated Ellen's first two weeks as a successful entrepreneur. Before the night was over, they had consumed 4 bottles of champagne.

Saturday, June 13:

i. Ellen went through the mail and noted that she had received payment in full from the Braverman/Liu wedding.
ii. She paid the balance owed to the vendors for both Braverman/Liu and Nickels/King (checks #206—#212).
iii. Before heading home, she reviewed the invoices received for the Clarke/O'Neil wedding and placed the billing statement in the mail (*Exhibit 2.3c*). She again held off on paying the vendors.

[5] For purposes of the discount, assume that the 10-day period begins at the time of title transfer, and the discount applies to the merchandise only (and not the shipping charge).

Monday, June 15:

i. Ellen received payments totaling $7,000 from the Nickels/King wedding. She called the groom and explained that until she received the full balance owed, she would do no further work on the project.
ii. She mailed the billing statement for the Daniel/Chan wedding (*Exhibit 2.3d*), but continued to hold off on paying the vendors.

Thursday, June 18:

i. The father of the bride brought in the balance due for the Nickels/King wedding.
ii. Ellen paid the balance owed to the Clarke/O'Neil vendors (voiding check #213 and utilizing checks #214—#219).

Monday, June 22:

The "meet & greet" promotional event was a great success with nine newly-engaged couples in attendance. Ellen felt that she had connected well with three of the couples and asked Sherri to slyly send them each home with a complimentary bottle of AA2R champagne.

Friday, June 26:

i. Ellen paid administrative assistant Sherri her $800 salary for the second two-week pay period (check #220).
ii. It had been a busy week, but the Nickels/King wedding went off without a hitch. Ellen realized she was behind on her bills. She prepared the final cost summary and billing statement for Nickels/King (*Exhibit 2.3e.*) and placed it in the mail.
iii. Wanting to maintain strong vendor relations, she paid the amount owed for Nickels/King and Daniels/Chan (checks #221—#226). She then turned her attention back to the Braverman/Liu wedding, which was in just a few hours.

Monday, June 29:

i. With the Braverman/Liu event successfully behind her, Ellen caught up on her office work.
   a. She decided to start charging a much higher fee for customers that give her less than 45 days notice to plan their event.
   b. She called the Clarke/O'Neil family to check some wedding details and to subtly remind them about their payment.
   c. She paid the bills for the "meet & greet" as follows:

Food & Beverage	$950 (check #227)
Flowers	$175 (check #228)
Harpist (2 hours)	$345 (check #229)

d. She sent Sherri shopping for more office supplies and spent the rest of the day putting some finishing touches on the Clarke/O'Neill July 4 extravaganza.

Tuesday, June 30:

i. Ellen reimbursed Sherri $350 for the office supplies she purchased (check #230), and after a conversation with her husband Dave, she made a $5,000 deposit toward a 10-day cruise to celebrate their 35th wedding anniversary (check #231). Although it seemed strange to pay a personal expense out of the business checking account, Ellen was proud to admit that it had been an exceptional first month and as the sole owner of AA2R, she was entitled to take home a share of the profits.

ii. Ellen sorted through the final invoices for the Braverman/Liu wedding. She called a few vendors and asked them to fax their final invoices. She hoped to finalize her numbers and get bills out by the end of the week.

iii. Ellen's intuition about the couples at the "meet & greet" was on target. The month ended with her holding initial consultations with two of the couples who were in attendance. Although signed contracts have yet to be received, Ellen feels extremely confident that fee deposits and contracts will be received within a few days.

Contract Date	Wedding Date	Countdown	Bride/Groom	Consultant Fee	Initial Budget
06/30/09	10/10/10	463 days	White/Feldman	$15,000	$180,000
06/30/09	11/11/11	860 days	Davis/Kinsella	$23,500	$225,000

Exhibit 2.3a: June Client Billing Statement

An Affair to Remember

Couple:
Lauren Nickels & David King

1218 S. Fayette Street
Alexandria, VA 22314

Proprietor: Mrs. Ellen Litchfield

"fully devoted to helping you achieve the wedding of your dreams"

Event Date: 6/20/2009

Statement Date: 6/11/2009

Payment due upon receipt

	Actual Cost	Budgeted
Invitations	$225.00	$160.00
Website	75.00	75.00
Reception Favors	325.00	250.00
Wedding Party Gifts	250.00	300.00
Flowers	2,200.00	1,600.00
Photographer	1,100.00	2,200.00
Videographer	550.00	1,100.00
Wedding Dress	1,800.00	1,100.00
Music	400.00	800.00
Cake	450.00	400.00
Reception Fees	250.00	250.00
Food		4,000.00
Alcohol		400.00
Reception Extras	300.00	300.00
Transportation	150.00	300.00
Accommodations		185.00
Officiant Fees		125.00
Other		455.00
	$8,075.00	$14,000.00
Handling Fee	202.00	
Amount Due	$8,277.00	

*See *Exhibit 2.1* for additional clarification regarding the accounting treatment of "contract services."

Exhibit 2.3b: June Client Billing Statement

An Affair to Remember

Couple:
Kim Braverman & Stephen Liu

1218 S. Fayette Street
Alexandria, VA 22314

Proprietor: Mrs. Ellen Litchfield

"fully devoted to helping you achieve the wedding of your dreams"

Event Date: 6/27/2009

Statement Date: 6/11/2009

Payment due upon receipt

	Actual Cost	Budgeted
Invitations	$570.00	$460.00
Website	75.00	75.00
Reception Favors	400.00	650.00
Wedding Party Gifts		
Flowers	850.00	1,900.00
Photographer	1,100.00	2,200.00
Videographer	550.00	1,100.00
Wedding Dress	2,200.00	1,600.00
Music	700.00	1,100.00
Cake	300.00	750.00
Reception Fees	250.00	250.00
Food		5,500.00
Alcohol		1,600.00
Reception Extras		
Transportation	150.00	300.00
Accommodations		225.00
Officiant Fees		125.00
Other	145.00	165.00
	$7,290.00	$18,000.00
Handling Fee	182.00	
Amount Due	$7,472.00	

*See *Exhibit 2.1* for additional clarification regarding the accounting treatment of "contract services."

Exhibit 2.3c: June Client Billing Statement

An Affair to Remember

Couple:
Kelly Clarke & John O'Neil

1218 S. Fayette Street
Alexandria, VA 22314

Proprietor: Mrs. Ellen Litchfield

"fully devoted to helping you achieve the wedding of your dreams"

Event Date: 7/4/2009

Statement Date: 6/13/2009

Payment due upon receipt

	Actual Cost	Budgeted
Invitations	$1,400.00	$1,575.00
Website	75.00	75.00
Reception Favors	1,800.00	1,500.00
Wedding Party Gifts	300.00	
Flowers	2,100.00	4,200.00
Photographer	1,100.00	2,200.00
Videographer	550.00	1,100.00
Wedding Dress	4,675.00	4,500.00
Music	3,250.00	7,500.00
Cake	1,000.00	1,800.00
Reception Fees	300.00	300.00
Food		13,000.00
Alcohol		5,800.00
Reception Extras	500.00	700.00
Transportation	125.00	300.00
Accommodations		325.00
Officiant Fees		125.00
Other	160.00	
	$17,335.00	$45,000.00
Handling Fee	433.00	
Amount Due	$17,768.00	

*See *Exhibit 2.1* for additional clarification regarding the accounting treatment of "contract services."

Exhibit 2.3d: June Client Billing Statement

An Affair to Remember

Couple:
Samantha Daniel & Lee Chan

1218 S. Fayette Street
Alexandria, VA 22314

Proprietor: Mrs. Ellen Litchfield

"fully devoted to helping you achieve the wedding of your dreams"

Event Date: 7/25/2009

Statement Date: 6/15/2009

Payment due upon receipt

	Actual Cost	Budgeted
Invitations	$1,475.00	$1,800.00
Website	75.00	75.00
Reception Favors		2,200.00
Wedding Party Gifts		900.00
Flowers	1,800.00	3,600.00
Photographer	1,100.00	2,200.00
Videographer	600.00	1,100.00
Wedding Dress	5,500.00	3,800.00
Music	2,200.00	4,500.00
Cake	750.00	1,450.00
Reception Fees	350.00	350.00
Food		9,500.00
Alcohol		3,400.00
Reception Extras		310.00
Transportation		300.00
Accommodations		225.00
Officiant Fees		125.00
Other	125.00	165.00
	$13,975.00	$36,000.00
Handling Fee	349.00	
Amount Due	$14,324.00	

*See *Exhibit 2.1* for additional clarification regarding the accounting treatment of "contract services."

Exhibit 2.3e: June Client Billing Statement

An Affair to Remember

Couple:
Lauren Nickels & David King

Event Date: 6/20/2009

Statement Date: 6/26/2009

Payment due upon receipt

1218 S. Fayette Street
Alexandria, VA 22314

Proprietor: Mrs. Ellen Litchfield

"fully devoted to helping you achieve the wedding of your dreams"

	Actual Cost			
	through June 11	June 12- June 20	Total	Budgeted Cost
Invitations	$225.00		$225.00	$160.00
Website	75.00		75.00	75.00
Reception Favors	325.00		325.00	250.00
Wedding Party	250.00		250.00	300.00
Flowers	2,200.00	900.00	3,100.00	1,600.00
Photographer	1,100.00	1,100.00	2,200.00	2,200.00
Videographer	550.00	550.00	1,100.00	1,100.00
Wedding Dress	1,800.00	275.00	2,075.00	1,100.00
Music	400.00	650.00	1,050.00	800.00
Cake	450.00	325.00	775.00	400.00
Reception Fees	250.00		250.00	250.00
Food		5,600.00	5,600.00	4,000.00
Alcohol		900.00	900.00	400.00
Reception Extras	300.00		300.00	300.00
Transportation	150.00		150.00	300.00
Accommodations		189.00	189.00	185.00
Officiant Fees		125.00	125.00	125.00
Other		725.00	725.00	455.00
	$8,075.00	$11,339.00	$19,414.00	$14,000.00
Handling Fee	202.00	283.00	485.00	
Amount Due	$8,277.00	$11,622.00	$19,899.00	
Paid: 6/15	(7,000.00)		(7,000.00)	
Paid: 6/18	(1,277.00)		(1,277.00)	
Balance	$ 0.00	$11,622.00	$11,622.00	

*See *Exhibit 2.1* for additional clarification regarding the accounting treatment of "contract services."

Exhibit 2.4: Summary of July 2009 Events

Wednesday, July 1:

Ellen made it to the office early. With only three days left until the Clarke/O'Neil wedding, there was much to do.

i. At 2:00 p.m., she met with the bride Kelly Clarke and her family to go over some final details. Before leaving, Ellen asked about their outstanding account balance. Mr. Clarke explained that he had dropped off a $17,768 check the day before and had given it to Sherri. Sherri later confirmed that she had received the check and deposited it on Tuesday when leaving work.
ii. While at the office Ellen did a quick inventory of the supply closet noting that approximately $1,500 of the office supplies remained on hand. She quickly pulled together a shopping list for Sherri to replenish their stock and headed off to meet with the Clarke's caterer and florist.

Thursday, July 2:

Ellen prepared the final billing for the Braverman/ Liu wedding and placed it in to the mail (*Exhibit 2.5a*).

Friday, July 3:

Ellen's new copy machine/fax/printer was delivered. With all the craziness surrounding the Clarke/O'Neil wedding, she had forgotten entirely about placing the order! The invoice totaled $400. Included in the $400 was $45 of "white glove" shipping (which provides for both installation and initial setup). Ellen was pleasantly surprised to find that the copier had been shipped (FOB Shipping Point) on June 29, just a few hours after she placed her order!

Monday, July 6:

Ellen decided to heed her husband's warning (*Exhibit 2.2*, 6/2 (ii)) about the high price of the office furniture. She called the company and arranged to return all of the furniture for a full refund. This task was made easier by the fact that the furniture was still packaged from when it was delivered. Additionally, Ellen went through her mail and noted the following:

i. The utility bill for June totaling $375.
ii. The June Bank Statement.
   - Students who will not be required to complete ***Case 2-3*** should incorporate *Exhibit TN 2.2* here and prepare all entries that should be made as a result of the information provided in this exhibit.
   - Students who will be required to complete ***Case 2-3*** should move on with the problem. All entries that should be made as a result of reconciling the June bank statement will be recorded in ***Case 2-3***.

iii. Ellen gladly welcomed what was enclosed in the next letter she opened. The Davis/Kinsella wedding party had sent in their deposit in full to lock in her services for their 11/11/11 wedding extravaganza (*Exhibit 2.2*, 6/30(iii)).
iv. The local radio station sent her a June statement noting that 10 of the 50 advertising spots had run in June (*Exhibit 2.2*, 6/3 (iv)).
v. Daniels/Chan paid their $14,324 account balance (*Exhibit 2.3d*).

Wednesday, July 8:

Ellen prepared the final bill summary for the Clarke/O'Neil wedding (*Exhibit 2.5b*) and an interim billing statement for the Daniel/Chan wedding (*Exhibit 2.5c*).

Friday, July 10:

i. Ellen paid administrative assistant Sherri her $800 salary for the 10-day pay period ending on Friday, July 10 (*Exhibit 2.2*, 5/11(i)).
ii. Ellen paid the $15,760 balance due to the Braverman/Liu wedding vendors (*Exhibit 2.4*, 7/2).
iii. The photographer delivered the wedding album for Nickels/King and for Braverman/Liu couples. Ellen left a phone message for the newly-wedded Mrs. King informing her that she would deliver the album once payment was received in full. She notified the photographer not to release any photos to the family. Before leaving her office to deliver the album to Mr. & Mrs. Liu, she went to the supply closet to grab a bottle of champagne (*Exhibit 2.2*, 6/3 (iii)) and was horrified to discover that some of the boxes were entirely empty! She then went directly to speak with Sherri and was disappointed to hear that since the impromptu party on 6/12 (*Exhibit 2.2*), Sherri had occasionally been "sipping" in the afternoon while Ellen was out of the office. After Sherri's admittance, Ellen was harsh in her reprimand, but indicated her ultimate support of Sherri. Ellen requested that Sherri seek professional help in order to keep her job and wrote up a formal notice of disciplinary action, placing it in Sherri's employment file. Sherri promised that she would repay every penny. Upon further investigation, Ellen determined that Sherri's drinking was more than "occasional sipping." In fact, 19 bottles of champagne were missing. It appears that Sherri had been drinking one bottle per workday since the party![6]
iv. After a meeting with her accountant, Ellen personally paid back the money used for the cruise deposit as well as the cost of the 4 bottles of champagne from the party on 6/12 (*Exhibit 2.2*, 6/12(iii) and 6/30(i)). During this meeting, it was also decided that all equipment (office or otherwise) will be depreciated straight-line over 60 months (*Exhibit 2.2*, 6/1(i)(d)). Although Ellen hopes to keep the van (*Exhibit 2.2*, 6/1 (iv)) for at least 5 years, she recognizes that it is hard to predict as her travel varies quite significantly by client. She does know that she wants to keep the van "looking nice" and will trade it in when it reaches 45,000 miles, no matter how much time has passed. Because of this, her accountant determined that the van should be depreciated using the units-of-production method.[7]

[6] That is, from June 15-July 9, Sherri drank one bottle per day for nineteen workdays straight.
[7] Ellen drove the van 500 miles in June and 800 miles in July.

Exhibit 2.5a: July Client Billing Statement

An Affair to Remember

Couple:
Kim Braverman & Stephen Liu

Event Date: 6/27/2009

Statement Date: 7/2/2009

Payment due upon receipt

1218 S. Fayette Street
Alexandria, VA 22314

Proprietor: Mrs. Ellen Litchfield

"fully devoted to helping you achieve the wedding of your dreams"

	Actual Cost			
	through June 11	June 12- June 27	Total	Budgeted Cost
Invitations	$570.00		$570.00	$460.00
Website	75.00		75.00	75.00
Reception Favors	400.00	350.00	750.00	650.00
Wedding Party		350.00	350.00	
Flowers	850.00	1,525.00	2,375.00	1,900.00
Photographer	1,100.00		1,100.00	2,200.00
Videographer	550.00		550.00	1,100.00
Wedding Dress	2,200.00	275.00	2,475.00	1,600.00
Music	700.00	900.00	1,600.00	1,100.00
Cake	300.00	850.00	1,150.00	750.00
Reception Fees	250.00		250.00	250.00
Food		6,400.00	6,400.00	5,500.00
Alcohol		4,400.00	4,400.00	1,600.00
Reception Extras		325.00	325.00	
Transportation	150.00	15.00	165.00	300.00
Accommodations		245.00	245.00	225.00
Officiant Fees		125.00	125.00	125.00
Other	145.00	________	145.00	165.00
	$7,290.00	$15,760.00	$23,050.00	$18,000.00
Handling Fee	182.00	395.00	577.00	
Amount Due	$7,472.00	$16,155.00	$23,627.00	
Paid: 6/13	(7,472.00)	________	(7,472.00)	
Balance Due	$ 0.00	$16,155.00	$16,155.00	

*See *Exhibit 2.1* for additional clarification regarding the accounting treatment of "contract services."

Exhibit 2.5b: July Client Billing Statement

An Affair to Remember

Couple:
Kelly Clarke & John O'Neil

Event Date: 7/4/2009

Statement Date: 7/8/2009

Payment due upon receipt

1218 S. Fayette Street
Alexandria, VA 22314

Proprietor: Mrs. Ellen Litchfield

"fully devoted to helping you achieve the wedding of your dreams"

	Actual Cost				
	through June 13	June 14-June 30	July 1-July 4	Total	Budgeted Cost
Invitations	$1,400.00			$1,400.00	$1,575.00
Website	75.00			75.00	75.00
Reception Favors	1,800.00	425.00		2,225.00	1,500.00
Wedding Party Gifts	300.00	350.00		650.00	
Flowers	2,100.00		3,000.00	5,100.00	4,200.00
Photographer	1,100.00		1,100.00	2,200.00	2,200.00
Videographer	550.00	550.00		1,100.00	1,100.00
Wedding Dress	4,675.00	275.00		4,950.00	4,500.00
Music	3,250.00	4,550.00		7,800.00	7,500.00
Cake	1,000.00	850.00		1,850.00	1,800.00
Reception Fees	300.00			300.00	300.00
Food		11,500.00	3,600.00	15,100.00	13,000.00
Alcohol		4,400.00	2,800.00	7,200.00	5,800.00
Reception Extras	500.00	225.00		725.00	700.00
Transportation	125.00	175.00		300.00	300.00
Accommodations		325.00		325.00	325.00
Officiant Fees		125.00		125.00	125.00
Other	160.00			160.00	
	$17,335.00	$23,750.00	$10,500.00	$51,585.00	$45,000.00
Handling Fee	433.00	580.00	275.00	1,288.00	
Amount Due	$17,768.00	$24,330.00	$10,775.00	$52,873.00	
Paid: 6/30	(17,768.00)			(17,768.00)	
Balance Due	$ 0.00	$24,330.00	$10,775.00	$35,105.00	

*See *Exhibit 2.1* for additional clarification regarding the accounting treatment of "contract services."

Exhibit 2.5c: July Client Billing Statement

An Affair to Remember

Couple:
Samantha Daniel & Lee Chan

1218 S. Fayette Street
Alexandria, VA 22314

Proprietor: Mrs. Ellen Litchfield

"fully devoted to helping you achieve the wedding of your dreams"

Event Date: 7/25/2009

Statement Date: 7/8/2009

Payment due upon receipt

	Actual Cost				
	through June 15	June 16-June 30	July 1-July 7	Total	Budgeted Cost
Invitations	$1,475.00			$1,475.00	$1,800.00
Website	75.00			75.00	75.00
Reception Favors		900.00	1,900.00	2,800.00	2,200.00
Wedding Party Gifts		1,100.00		1,100.00	900.00
Flowers	1,800.00		1,500.00	3,300.00	3,600.00
Photographer	1,100.00			1,100.00	2,200.00
Videographer	600.00			600.00	1,100.00
Wedding Dress	5,500.00		475.00	5,975.00	3,800.00
Music	2,200.00			2,200.00	4,500.00
Cake	750.00	500.00		1,250.00	1,450.00
Reception Fees	350.00			350.00	350.00
Food				0.00	9,500.00
Alcohol				0.00	3,400.00
Reception Extras		275.00	185.00	460.00	310.00
Transportation		150.00		150.00	300.00
Accommodations		25.00		25.00	225.00
Officiant Fees				0.00	125.00
Other	125.00		25.00	150.00	165.00
	$13,975.00	$2,950.00	$4,085.00	$21,010.00	$36,000.00
Handling Fee	349.00	90.00	115.00	554.00	
Amount Due	$14,324.00	$3,040.00	$4,200.00	$21,564.00	
Paid: 7/6	(14,324.00)			(14,324.00)	
Balance Due	$ 0.00	$3,040.00	$4,200.00	$ 7,240.00	

*See *Exhibit 2.1* for additional clarification regarding the accounting treatment of "contract services."

Exhibit 2.6a: The June Bank Statement

(prepared by the bank)

American Bank
600 North Washington Street
Alexandria, VA 22314

An Affair to Remember
1218 S. Fayette Street
Alexandria, VA 22314

Statement Date: 6/30/2009
Account # 28569

Account Summary:

Week Ending	Deposit	Withdrawal	Balance
31-May			$ 0.00
7-Jun	52,800.00	26,550.00	26,250.00
14-Jun	10,000.00	12,837.20	23,412.80
21-Jun	15,749.00	18,535.00	20,626.80
28-Jun	-	16,852.00	3,774.80
30-Jun	25,000.00	11,055.00	17,719.80
	$103,549.00	$85,829.20	

DATE	**Checks **	
3-Jun	No. 200	$10,800.00
	No. 201	2,400.00
	No. 202	7,000.00
	No. 203	600.00
11-Jun	No. 204	625.00
15-Jun	No. 210	1,100.00
16-Jun	No. 205	800.00
	No. 207	3,450.00
	No. 208	750.00
	No. 212	300.00
18-Jun	No. 206	3,050.00
	No. 211	250.00
22-Jun	No. 214	2,100.00
	No. 216	1,000.00
23-Jun	No. 215	1,725.00
	No. 218	125.00
26-Jun	No. 217	3,250.00
29-Jun	No. 222	3,425.00
	No. 226	125.00
30-Jun	No. 223	1,075.00
	No. 224	2,580.00

Deposits & Other Credits

Date	Type	Amount
1-Jun	DEP	45,000.00
3-Jun	DEP	3,000.00
5-Jun	DEP	4,800.00
11-Jun	DEP	6,500.00
13-Jun	DEP	3,500.00
15-Jun	DEP	7,472.00
16-Jun	DEP	7,000.00
19-Jun	DEP	1,277.00
29-Jun	LOC	15,000.00*
30-Jun	LOC	10,000.00*

Other Debits

Date	Type	Payee	Amount
3-Jun	DC	*The Daily Post*	1,500.00
	DC	*WPQS Radio*	4,250.00
10-Jun	DC	*Gift Specialties*	4,880.00
	DC	*Forever Wed*	1,117.20
13-Jun	DC	*Allure Bridal*	4,000.00
	DC	*Forever Wed*	2,215.00
18-Jun	DC	*Allure Bridal*	4,675.00
	DC	*Forever Wed*	4,160.00
22-Jun	NSF		1,277.00*
26-Jun	DC	*Allure Bridal*	5,775.00
	DC	*Forever Wed*	1,600.00
30-Jun		*LLSM Finance Co*	400.00*
	DC	Bolder Image	3,425.00
	SC		25.00

KEY:	
SC	Service Charge
DC	Debit Card Purchase
LOC	Line of Credit Borrowings
INT	Interest Income
NSF	Insufficient funds

American Bank- June 30 Bank Statement page 1 of 8

*See *Exhibit 2.6b* for more details concerning these items

An Affair to Remember
1218 S. Fayette Street
Alexandria, Virginia

#200

Date 6/1/2009

Pay to the order of Harmon Real Estate $ 10,800 —

American Bank- 600 North Washington Street, Alexandria, VA 22314

Memo ______________ Signature: Ellen Litchfield

1: 068674830¶28569¶0200

An Affair to Remember
1218 S. Fayette Street
Alexandria, Virginia

#201

Date 6/1/2009

Pay to the order of State Farm Insurance $ 2,400 —

American Bank- 600 North Washington Street, Alexandria, VA 22314

Memo ______________ Signature: Ellen Litchfield

1: 068674830¶28569¶0201

An Affair to Remember
1218 S. Fayette Street
Alexandria, Virginia

#202

Date 6/1/2009

Pay to the order of Alexandria Plaza $ 7,000 —

American Bank- 600 North Washington Street, Alexandria, VA 22314

Memo ______________ Signature: Ellen Litchfield

1: 068674830¶28569¶0202

American Bank- June 30 Bank Statement page 2 of 8

An Affair to Remember
1218 S. Fayette Street
Alexandria, Virginia

#203

Date 6/1/2009

Pay to the order of State Farm Insurance $ 600 —

American Bank- 600 North Washington Street, Alexandria, VA 22314

Memo

Signature: Ellen Litchfield

1: 06867483012856910203

An Affair to Remember
1218 S. Fayette Street
Alexandria, Virginia

#204

Date 6/8/2009

Pay to the order of U.S. Post master $ 625.00

American Bank- 600 North Washington Street, Alexandria, VA 22314

Memo

Signature: Ellen Litchfield

1: 068674830¶28569¶0204

An Affair to Remember
1218 S. Fayette Street
Alexandria, Virginia

#210

Date 6/13/2009

Pay to the order of EB Talent $ 1,100 —

American Bank- 600 North Washington Street, Alexandria, VA 22314

Memo

Signature: Ellen Litchfield

1: 068674830¶28569¶0210

American Bank- June 30 Bank Statement page 3 of 8

An Affair to Remember
1218 S. Fayette Street
Alexandria, Virginia

#205

Date 6/12/2009

Pay to the order of Sheri Loveless $ 800 —

American Bank- 600 North Washington Street, Alexandria, VA 22314

Memo

Signature: Ellen Litchfield

1: 0686748301128569¶0205

An Affair to Remember
1218 S. Fayette Street
Alexandria, Virginia

#207

Date 6/13/2009

Pay to the order of Golden Image $ 3,450 —

American Bank- 600 North Washington Street, Alexandria, VA 22314

Memo

Signature: Ellen Litchfield

1: 068674830¶28569¶0207

An Affair to Remember
1218 S. Fayette Street
Alexandria, Virginia

#208

Date 6/13/2009

Pay to the order of Cake Artist Studio $ 750 —

American Bank- 600 North Washington Street, Alexandria, VA 22314

Memo

Signature: Ellen Litchfield

1: 068674830¶28569¶0208

American Bank- June 30 Bank Statement page 4 of 8

#212

An Affair to Remember
1218 S. Fayette Street
Alexandria, Virginia

Date 6/13/2009

Pay to the order of Luxe Limo Service $ 300 —

American Bank- 600 North Washington Street, Alexandria, VA 22314

Memo

Signature: Ellen Litchfield

1: 068674830¶28569¶0212

#206

An Affair to Remember
1218 S. Fayette Street
Alexandria, Virginia

Date 6/13/2009

Pay to the order of Art Floral $ 3,050 —

American Bank- 600 North Washington Street, Alexandria, VA 22314

Memo

Signature: Ellen Litchfield

1: 068674830¶28569¶0206

#211

An Affair to Remember
1218 S. Fayette Street
Alexandria, Virginia

Date 6/13/2009

Pay to the order of Hyatt Regency $ 250 —

American Bank- 600 North Washington Street, Alexandria, VA 22314

Memo

Signature: Ellen Litchfield

1: 068674830¶28569¶0211

American Bank- June 30 Bank Statement page 5 of 8

An Affair to Remember
1218 S. Fayette Street
Alexandria, Virginia

#214

Date 6/18/2009

Pay to the order of Art Floral $ 2,100 —

American Bank- 600 North Washington Street, Alexandria, VA 22314

Memo ______________ Signature: Ellen Litchfield

1: 068674830¶28569¶0214

An Affair to Remember
1218 S. Fayette Street
Alexandria, Virginia

#216

Date 6/18/2009

Pay to the order of Cake Artist Studio $ 1,000 —

American Bank- 600 North Washington Street, Alexandria, VA 22314

Memo ______________ Signature: Ellen Litchfield

1: 068674830¶28569¶0216

An Affair to Remember
1218 S. Fayette Street
Alexandria, Virginia

#215

Date 6/18/2009

Pay to the order of Bolder Image $ 4,725 —

American Bank- 600 North Washington Street, Alexandria, VA 22314

Memo ______________ Signature: Ellen Litchfield

1: 068674830¶28569¶0215

American Bank- June 30 Bank Statement page 6 of 8

#218

An Affair to Remember
1218 S. Fayette Street
Alexandria, Virginia

Date 6/18/2009

Pay to the order of Luxe Limo Service $ 125 —

American Bank- 600 North Washington Street, Alexandria, VA 22314

Memo

Signature: Ellen Litchfield

1: 068674830¶28569¶0218

#217

An Affair to Remember
1218 S. Fayette Street
Alexandria, Virginia

Date 6/18/2009

Pay to the order of E B Talent $ 3,250 —

American Bank- 600 North Washington Street, Alexandria, VA 22314

Memo

Signature: Ellen Litchfield

1: 068674830¶28569¶0217

#222

An Affair to Remember
1218 S. Fayette Street
Alexandria, Virginia

Date 6/26/2009

Pay to the order of Bolder Image $ 3425 —

American Bank- 600 North Washington Street, Alexandria, VA 22314

Memo

Signature: Ellen Litchfield

1: 068674830¶28569¶0222

American Bank- June 30 Bank Statement page 7 of 8

An Affair to Remember
1218 S. Fayette Street
Alexandria, Virginia

#226

Date 6/26/2009

Pay to the order of Saint Mark Catholic Church $ 125 —

American Bank- 600 North Washington Street, Alexandria, VA 22314

Memo ____________ Signature: Ellen Litchfield

1: 0686748301285691 0226

An Affair to Remember
1218 S. Fayette Street
Alexandria, Virginia

#223

Date 6/26/2009

Pay to the order of Cake Artist Studio $ 4,075 —

American Bank- 600 North Washington Street, Alexandria, VA 22314

Memo ____________ Signature: Ellen Litchfield

1: 0686748301285691 0223

An Affair to Remember
1218 S. Fayette Street
Alexandria, Virginia

#224

Date 6/26/2009

Pay to the order of EB Talent $ 2,850 —

American Bank- 600 North Washington Street, Alexandria, VA 22314

Memo ____________ Signature: Ellen Litchfield

1: 0686748301285691 0224

American Bank- June 30 Bank Statement page 8 of 8

Exhibit 2.6b: Details of Items Noted in June Bank Statement (*Exhibit 2.6a*)

I. NSF

The $1,277 check received on 6/18 from Nickels/King (*Exhibit 2.2*) was shown as NSF! That is, when American Bank presented the check payment to the Mr. Nickels' bank, it was notified that the check could not be honored due to the existence of insufficient funds in his account. Ellen immediately tried to call her banker to inquire why she had not received notification before now. Certainly, she had not overlooked a notice in the mail regarding this bounced check! Either way, she was quite upset to discover this almost 20 days later. After not being able to reach Mr. Nickels by phone, she quickly thought to call her attorney who, in turn, promptly mailed Mr. Nickels a letter requesting that he pay the entire balance due within 72 hours. Ellen was pleased to note that her attorney had copied the groom's family on the letter.

II. LLSM Finance Co.

The bank statement reported that on June 30, her first $400 auto loan payment ($310 of which was considered principal) had been withdrawn from the account. At the time she signed the loan paperwork, she gave the finance company (LLSM Finance) permission to automatically withdraw the payment from her checking account (*Exhibit 2.2*, 6/1(iv)).

III. LOC

The bank statement showed that on June 29, the line of credit (LOC) was needed to cover the cash overdraft and $15,000 was deposited into the account. On June 30, an additional $10,000 was deposited into the account from the line of credit.

Exhibit 2.7: Ellen's Summary Schedules (p. 1 of 4)

Note: If you encounter a discrepancy between the checkbook and the bank statement, please note that the numbers reported in this exhibit (prepared by Ellen) are correct and do not contain errors. That is, the cost summaries provided in *Exhibit 2.7* accurately represent (i) all wedding costs incurred to date, and (ii) all vendor payments made (and authorized by Ellen) during the month of June.

	Nickels/ King	**Braverman/ Liu**	**Clarke/ O'Neil**	**Daniels/ Chan**	**White/ Feldman**	**Davis/ Kinsella**
Client #	62009	62709	70409	72509	101010	111111
Contract Date	6/2/2009	6/2/2009	6/4/2009	6/12/2009	6/30/2009	6/30/2009
Wedding Date	6/20/2009	6/27/2009	7/4/2009	7/25/2009	10/10/2010	11/11/2011
Total Count Down	18 days	25 Days	30 Days	43 Days	463 Days	860 Days
Consulting Fee Collected	$1,500	$1,500	$4,800	$3,500	$15,000	$23,500
Initial Wedding Budget	$14,000	$18,000	$45,000	$36,000	$180,000	$225,000
Actual Costs to Date	**$19,414**	**$7,290**	**$17,335**	**$13,975**		
Billing Statement #1:	*Exhibit 2.3a*	*Exhibit 2.3b*	*Exhibit 2.3c*	*Exhibit 2.3d*		
Billing Statement #2:	*Exhibit 2.3e*					
Client Payments:						
13-Jun		7,472				
15-Jun	7,000					
18-Jun	1,277					
30-Jun			17,768			
6-Jul				14,324		
Payments to Vendors:						
13-Jun	-8,075	-7,290				
18-Jun			-17,335			
26-Jun	-11,339			-13,975		
Total June Payments	**$19,414**	**$7,290**	**$17,335**	**$13,975**		

Exhibit 2.7: Ellen's Summary Schedules (p. 2 of 4)

June 13: Payment/Vendor Summary

Client #	Nickels/King 62009	Braverman/Liu 62709	Amount Owed	Vendor Name
Wedding Dress	$1,800.00	$2,200.00	$4,000.00	Allure Bridal
Flowers	2,200.00	850.00	3,050.00	Art Floral
Website	75.00	75.00	150.00	Bolder Image
Photographer	1,100.00	1,100.00	2,200.00	Bolder Image
Videographer	550.00	550.00	1,100.00	Bolder Image
Cake	450.00	300.00	750.00	Cake Artist Studio
Reception Fees		250.00	250.00	Country Club
Music	400.00	700.00	1,100.00	EB Talent
Reception Favors	325.00	400.00	725.00	Forever Wed
Wedding Party Gifts	250.00		250.00	Forever Wed
Reception Extras	300.00		300.00	Forever Wed
Invitations	225.00	570.00	795.00	Forever Wed
Other		145.00	145.00	Forever Wed
Reception Fees	250.00		250.00	Hyatt Regency
Transportation	150.00	150.00	300.00	Luxe Limo Service
	$8,075.00	$7,290.00	**$15,365.00**	

Check #		
*	Allure Bridal	$4,000.00
#206	Art Floral	3,050.00
#207	Bolder Image	3,450.00
#208	Cake Artist Studio	750.00
#209	Country Club	250.00
#210	EB Talent	1,100.00
*	Forever Wed	2,215.00
#211	Hyatt Regency	250.00
#212	Luxe Limo Service	300.00
		$15,365.00

* paid by debit card

Exhibit 2.7: Ellen's Summary Schedules (p. 3 of 4)

June 18: Payment/Vendor Summary

Clarke/O'Neil

#070409	Amount Owed	Vendor Name
Wedding Dress	$4,675.00	Allure Bridal
Flowers	2,100.00	Art Floral
Website	75.00	Bolder Image
Photographer	1,100.00	Bolder Image
Videographer	550.00	Bolder Image
Cake	1,000.00	Cake Artist Studio
Music	3,250.00	EB Talent
Reception Extras	500.00	Forever Wed
Invitations	1,400.00	Forever Wed
Reception Favors	1,800.00	Forever Wed
Wedding Party Gifts	300.00	Forever Wed
Transportation	125.00	Luxe Limo Service
Reception Fees	300.00	The Old Lodge
Other	160.00	Forever Wed
	$17,335.00	

Check #		
*	Allure Bridal	$4,675.00
#214	Art Floral	2,100.00
#215	Bolder Image	1,725.00
#216	Cake Artist Studio	1,000.00
#217	EB Talent	3,250.00
*	Forever Wed	4,160.00
#218	Luxe Limo Service	125.00
#219	The Olde Lodge	300.00
		$17,335.00

* paid by debit card

Exhibit 2.7: Ellen's Summary Schedules (p. 4 of 4)

June 26: Payment/Vendor Summary

Client #	Daniel/Chan 72509	Nickels/King 62009	Amount Owed	Vendor Name
Wedding Dress	$5,500.00	275.00	$5,775.00	Allure Bridal
Flowers	1,800.00	900.00	2,700.00	Art Floral
Website	75.00		75.00	Bolder Image
Photographer	1,100.00	1,100.00	2,200.00	Bolder Image
Videographer	600.00	550.00	1,150.00	Bolder Image
Cake	750.00	325.00	1,075.00	Cake Artist Studio
Music	2,200.00	650.00	2,850.00	EB Talent
Invitations	1,475.00		1,475.00	Forever Wed
Other	125.00		125.00	Forever Wed
Reception Fees	350.00		350.00	Hyatt Regency
Food		5,600.00	5,600.00	Hyatt Regency
Alcohol		900.00	900.00	Hyatt Regency
Accommodations		189.00	189.00	Hyatt Regency
Other		725.00	725.00	Hyatt Regency
Officiant Fees	______	125.00	125.00	SMCC
	$13,975.00	$11,339.00	**$25,314.00**	

Check #		
*	Allure Bridal	$5,775.00
#221	Art Floral	2,700.00
#222	Bolder Image	3,425.00
#223	Cake Artist Studio	1,075.00
#224	EB Talent	2,850.00
*	Forever Wed	1,600.00
#225	Hyatt Regency	7,764.00
#226	SMCC	125.00
		$25,314.00

* paid by debit card

Julia Shapland and Cynthia Turner

Project Orthodontist

Dr. Tamera Haines

3 Project Orthodontist

3 Project Orthodontist

Dr. Tamera Haines is an orthodontist in Lithia Springs, Georgia, who specializes in providing superior care for adults and children. She received her Bachelor of Science degree in Biology from Temple University in Philadelphia in 1999 and her Doctor of Dental Surgery degree (DDS) in 2004 from Howard University in Washington, DC. Dr. Haines is an active member of the American Association of Orthodontists, the American Dental Association, and the Georgia Dental Association.

A New York native, Dr. Haines currently resides in Lithia Springs, Georgia. She enjoys the theater, traveling, and spending time with her husband Stephen (an attorney) and their two young children.

The Orthodontic Practice

Dr. Haines has built a thriving orthodontic practice and its growth has been steady. As of November 30, 2010, Tamera had 525 cases in progress (as noted in *Figure 3.1*). Given the declining economy, she was pleased that this number represented only a slight decrease over the previous year.

Figure 3.1

Total Cases (1/1/10)	540
Cases Completed	(212)
New Cases Started	215
Transfers	(18)
Total Cases (11/30/10)	525

This course project was prepared by Julia P. Shapland and Cynthia W. Turner of the University of Illinois at Urbana-Champaign for classroom use and discussion. All businesses and characters appearing in this work are fictitious. Any resemblance to existing businesses or real persons, living or dead, is purely coincidental.

The orthodontic practice is located in the downtown district and is open from 8:30 a.m. to 5:30 p.m. on Tuesdays through Saturdays. Because of Dr. Haines' reputation, her services are in high demand. Accordingly, her schedule is usually full, and she often has a waiting list for premium times. Consequently, she allows her patients only two free missed appointments. After patients miss two appointments, she charges a $25 fee for any subsequent absence. This fee must be paid (in cash) at the time of the next appointment or treatment is suspended.

Dr. Haines has three experienced certified dental assistants who work for her. Their expertise allows her to see as many as 70 patients in a given day. As a result, she goes to great effort and expense to provide a competitive benefits package, and tries to keep the work environment pleasant for her staff. These efforts have not gone unnoticed, and other than the occasional maternity leave, her team has been with her since the opening of her practice. Because Dr. Haines believes "the best advertisement comes from a satisfied patient," she is grateful for the warm office environment maintained by her staff. She believes this atmosphere significantly contributes to her high retention and referral rates.

This year, Dr. Haines implemented a new program to reward her patients (and staff) for any new patient referral. So far, the program has been well-received and Dr. Haines plans to continue this promotion. Under the program, the individual making the referral can choose between receiving a $100 visa gift card or a $100 gift certificate to use toward his or her orthodontic treatment cost. The reward is received by the referring patient once the newly-referred patient has signed a contract and started treatment.

Patient Treatment

Consistent with the American Association of Orthodontists, Dr. Haines recommends that children receive their initial orthodontic evaluation no later than age 7. Depending on the findings of this evaluation, she may either postpone treatment or begin what is known as an interceptive treatment plan (ITP). By performing certain procedures early (before the adult teeth are fully erupted), an ITP can prevent certain problems from occurring and ultimately result in a shorter overall treatment time. Treatment times for typical cases range from 18 to 24 months. Her adult patients who did not benefit from an ITP may have more serious cases requiring longer, more extensive treatment plans.

Similar to industry practice, Dr. Haines offers the traditional metal bracket or "braces" for aligning teeth. However, the science of orthodontics has greatly advanced in recent years with new alternatives to traditional metal braces emerging and giving patients a variety of choices. Dr. Haines utilizes the latest technological advances in the industry and offers her patients choices such as invisible ceramic braces and Invisalign™. The cost of different types of braces—traditional metal, clear, and ceramic—can be a major factor in the decision of the type of bracket a patient eventually chooses. Depending on the nature of the treatment plan and the type of bracket that is chosen, treatment prices range from $5,000 to $7,000. As part of her patient support services, Dr. Haines uses the latest in computer technology (digital imaging and advanced computer graphics), ensuring that her patients receive the most effective care possible. Dr. Haines also generates a small amount of incidental revenue by selling Super Smile™ consumer whitening systems to interested patients. She makes bulk purchases of the systems throughout the year and keeps a sufficient supply of whitening systems on hand to meet patient demand. She sells the systems for $110 each and so far has received positive feedback back from her patients concerning these systems.

As a first step to beginning orthodontic treatment, the patient is given a free initial consultation by Dr. Haines. If it appears that the patient can benefit by immediately starting orthodontic treatment, Dr. Haines will discuss the treatment options with him or her. The patient will then meet with Paddy, the office manager, to discuss payment options. Paddy also provides the patient with a copy of the orthodontic treatment contract.

Cash Receipts, Cash Disbursements, and Delinquent Patient Accounts

Under the terms of the treatment contract, all patients (including those with insurance) are required to make an advance deposit covering the cost of the last three months of services. If a patient transfers or terminates his or her services, the deposit will be reimbursed. Dr. Haines recognizes that something as simple as a local business closing its doors can result in a sizable amount of patients having to terminate their treatment.

Accordingly, Dr. Haines invested $350,000 in a three-month CD at the local bank. Although the return is low, Dr. Haines feels more comfortable knowing that funds have been set aside should higher-than-normal deposit reimbursements be requested. When the CD matures, she plans to roll the funds over into another certificate with a similar term.

Dr. Haines understands that purchasing braces is a substantial financial investment, and in order to make high-quality orthodontic treatment affordable, she offers a variety of payment options. Virtually all patients choose the popular zero interest monthly payment plan because of its favorable terms. Once a patient is enrolled, monthly billings start with the second month of service. Patients are expected to pay when they are in the office for their regular monthly appointment. Although it is not a written policy, Dr. Haines is often generous about providing those patients who need it with some extra time to pay. She understands that orthodontic treatment is elective and is just one of many items competing for the family's disposable income. She finds that a little flexibility with payment terms may make the difference in whether or not a patient finishes treatment. Plus, she is confident in the abilities of her office manager Paddy. When it comes to collections, she considers Paddy her "secret weapon."

Paddy knows every patient by name and although she seems to spend much of her day "chatting it up" with the patients, she runs a tight ship. In particular, Paddy's "reconnaissance" proves incredibly useful when it comes to handling collections. Paddy possesses a keen sense of awareness that enables her to know when it is the right time to push a patient for collection and when the patient should be allowed a little more time. Once Paddy decides that a particular account should be paid, she is diligent about following up and can be firm with patients who she believes take advantage of Dr. Haines' kindness. It is not unusual for Paddy to drive on her lunch hour to the patient's house to pick up a payment. Although uncollectible accounts are unavoidable, Dr. Haines feels confident that when an account ultimately is written off, nothing more can be done.

Although most patients pay by cash, Dr. Haines also accepts Care Credit™, a revolving line of credit specifically used for health procedures not covered by insurance. About every ten days, the credit card company will deposit the amount owed (less a 3 percent service charge) directly into the business bank account.

Roughly 50 percent of Dr. Haines' patients have orthodontic insurance, which covers a small portion (usually 25 percent) of their treatment costs. Like patients without insurance, the remaining balance is paid at zero percent interest on a monthly basis. Dr. Haines expects the patients with insurance to pay their account balances at the time of the appointment and then seek reimbursement directly from their insurance companies.

After seeing Dr. Haines for an appointment, the patient is asked to take his or her chart to the front desk to check out. Upon looking at the chart, Carol, the receptionist, pulls up the patient's account on the computer system and verifies that there have been no changes in the patient's contact information. Dr. Haines uses the same practice management software to schedule appointments and to manage patient billing and receivables. The software tracks the account activity for each patient and represents the only detailed record of individual patient account balances.

After booking the next appointment, the payment, if any, is collected by Carol and the patient account on the computer system is updated. The software automatically prints an appointment card, and if requested to do so, Carol will also manually prepare a payment receipt. Before re-filing the patient treatment chart, Carol updates a payment history sheet contained in the patient file. Checks are restrictively endorsed before being locked in her desk drawer with the other funds collected. Carol updates a daily collection summary sheet that details all the payments received on a particular day. This summary sheet along with the cash, checks, and credit card receipts are provided to Paddy who then prepares a deposit ticket.

Paddy leaves work a few minutes early on Wednesdays and Saturdays to make the deposit. Paddy always makes a final deposit on the last day of the month even if it is not her regular deposit day. In the meantime, the deposit monies are kept locked in a safe in Dr. Haines private office. Only Paddy and Dr. Haines have the combination. Paddy accumulates the deposit tickets and provides them (along with the checkbook) to a local accounting firm which, in addition to handling payroll, prepares the monthly bank reconciliation.

As with any business, Dr. Haines has various recurring expenditures that are made each month. These items range from orthodontic supplies and payroll to occupancy costs such as rent, insurance, and utilities. Other than orthodontic supplies (which are always purchased on account from the same vendor Ortho Technologies), purchases are made by writing a check or charging the item on the corporate credit card. Dr. Haines keeps $100 of petty cash on hand for the occasional time that cash must be used to pay for something. Carol administers the petty cash and office policy requires that reimbursement of any expenditure must be approved by Paddy or Dr. Haines, and the original receipt must be submitted.

Dr. Haines does not use a computerized accounting software package, and Paddy maintains the underlying accounting records and checkbook by hand. In the past, Dr. Haines has not prepared any sort of formal financial statement. Instead, Paddy has prepared standalone reports and spreadsheets that are used by Dr. Haines' outside accountants to prepare the annual tax returns for the orthodontic practice.

This year things have changed. In early 2010, Dr. Haines' landlord Mr. Helm approached her about purchasing the building in which she currently rents office space. The building will be sold and if she doesn't buy it, the orthodontic practice will need to relocate. Dr. Haines appreciates the building's convenient, downtown location and the fact that it has plenty of parking. Her patients are familiar with the location, and the space works well for her needs. Consequently, she has moved forward to obtain a bank loan to finance the purchase. As part of the loan approval process, the bank has asked that she provide a complete set of accrual financial statements. Specifically, she must provide an Income Statement, a Statement of Equity, and a Statement of Cash Flow for the 12 months ended December 31, 2010 and a classified Balance Sheet dated as of December 31, 2010.

With the assistance of the outside accounting firm, Paddy has already recorded the monthly transactions for January through November and some, but not all of the required adjusting journal entries needed to prepare December financial statements.

Case 3-1

Classifying Financial Statement Elements

(and working with the balance sheet equation)

You have been provided with the following item:

- Exhibit 3.1: A listing of the individual account balances reported on Dr. Haines Orthodontic Practice's 11/30/10 trial balance. The balances shown in *Exhibit 3.1* are for the 11 months ended 11/30/10. All accounts have normal balances (that is, account balances that are expected to carry a debit balance have a debit balance and vice versa). Further, please note that this exhibit provides you with *a description* of the underlying account rather than an actual account title (such as Accounts Receivable, Accounts Payable, Rent Expense, and so on). Each description represents one single account from either the Balance Sheet (such as an asset, liability, or equity account) or from the Income Statement (in which it measures either revenues earned or expenses incurred from January through November 2010).

Requirements:

1. Use the ***Narrative*** to classify each account listed in *Exhibit 3.1* as an asset, liability, equity, revenue, or expense account. When submitting this requirement, please list the accounts in numeric order, using the account reference numbers provided in the first column of *Exhibit 3.1*.

2. Prepare an 11/30/10 trial balance using the figures provided in *Exhibit 3.1* and your account classification from requirement (1). The cash balance has been intentionally omitted from this listing. Please solve for the missing cash balance and include this amount in your trial balance. When submitting this requirement, please sort the accounts in numeric order using the account reference numbers provided in *Exhibit 3.1*.

3. Using your final trial balance from requirement (2), compute the following items (and show all work):

   a. Total equity as of 11/30/2010 (using the balance sheet equation).

   b. Net income for the 11 months ending 11/30/10.

4. Using the balance you computed for total equity in requirement (3a), determine how much of this balance is:

   a. Total contributed capital.

   b. Total retained earnings.

5. Please consider the account titled "Retained Earnings, January 1, 2010." What does this account balance communicate about 2009's financial performance? Why is this number different than your calculation for requirement (4b)? Explain.

Case 3-2

Analyzing Monthly Transactions

Your parents are close friends with Dr. Haines and her husband. In December, you graduated with your accounting degree and returned home for a short break before moving to Chicago to begin working for a national accounting firm. While home, you bumped into Dr. Haines at a holiday gathering. During the course of your conversation, she expressed both her delight and relief in seeing you because she was in a dilemma and thought that you might be able to assist. Paddy, her office manager, had recently become a grandmother. Because Paddy's grandchild was born earlier than expected, she had to leave town in a hurry and was unable to prepare the December financials. Dr. Haines lamented over the fact that she was in the midst of obtaining a loan and needed to provide 2010 financial statements to her loan officer. She was uncertain when Paddy would return to work, and being familiar with your choice of careers, she asked if you would consider helping her out while you were home. Welcoming the opportunity to stay busy and get out of the house, you quickly agreed to help.

In order to assist you in your work, Dr. Haines has provided you with the following items:

- Exhibit 3.2: Paddy's December notes. (Although Paddy did not record any December transactions, she did keep detailed notes regarding the transactions and events that took place in December.)
- Exhibits 3.3a and 3.3b: The December payroll records (from the outside accounting firm.)
- Exhibit 3.4: The daily collection summary sheet prepared by Carol, the receptionist.
- Exhibit TN 3.1: The 11/30/2010 trial balance ***(available from your instructor)***. *(These balances should be used as your beginning account balances.)*

Requirements:

1. Referring back to the ***Narrative*** as needed, please prepare journal entries (using good form) *as necessary* for the December transactions and events described in the accompanying exhibits for this case. That is, you should prepare only those *specific* entries required to

record the transactions described in these materials. You are not to consider adjusting entries that would be recorded after the events described in these exhibits.[1]

2. Using the journal entries that you prepared in requirement (1), post the entries to "T" accounts and calculate the overall account balances.

3. Using the ending balances in the "T" accounts from requirement (2), prepare a 12/31/10 unadjusted trial balance for Dr. Haines' orthodontic practice. Please provide a summary detailing *all* items you have recorded in "miscellaneous expense."

4. Consider whether any account balance in the unadjusted trial balance prepared in requirement (3) is abnormal. (That is, an account balance that is expected to carry a debit balance has a credit balance and vice versa.) If you determine that a particular account balance is abnormal, label it as such and explain what the abnormal balance communicates.

5. Briefly describe the prepaid insurance account, how it is used, and how it is different than the insurance expense account. Will a company that incurs insurance cost always have a prepaid insurance account? Explain.

6. Consider the December accounting thus far for the Super Smile Whitening Systems.[2] Do you feel that the "realization" and "matching" principles have been properly applied thus far? Is the recording of more entries needed during the adjustment process? If so, what additional information, if any, do you need? (Remember, you are not recording adjusting entries in this case.) Please discuss.

---

[1] Please use the account titles listed in *Exhibit TN 3.1* for purposes of your entries. If you need to create a new account, please do so, but clearly label it as to its type (that is, asset, liability, equity, revenue, or expense). You may also find it helpful to review the detailed descriptions of the 11/30 account balances contained in *Exhibit 3.1*.

[2] You may find *Exhibit 3.6* helpful when answering this question.

Case 3-3

Recording Year-End Adjustments

Having recently graduated with your accounting degree, you have agreed to assist family friend Dr. Tamera Haines while home on a short break. Paddy, her office manager, was out on extended vacation, and Dr. Haines needed assistance in preparing her practice's 2010 financial statements. To date, you have assisted Dr. Haines by recording her practice's December transactions, and you are now ready to prepare the December adjusting entries.

Dr. Haines provides the following items to assist you in preparing the year-end adjustments.

- *Exhibit 3.5*: Summary of events that took place during the first two weeks of January 2011.
- *Exhibit 3.6*: Super Smile 2010 Inventory Purchase Schedule.
- *Exhibit 3.7*: Invoice for the 50 Super Smile Whitening Systems delivered on 1/3/11.
- *Exhibit 3.8*: Carol's daily collection summary sheet for the first two weeks of January 2011.
- *Exhibitst 3.9a and 3.9b*: The January Payroll and 2010 Depreciation Schedule prepared by the outside accounting firm.
- *Exhibit 3.10*: The monthly billing for the corporate credit card.
- *Exhibit TN 3.2*: The 12/31/10 unadjusted trial balance for the orthodontic practice ***(available from your instructor)***. *(These balances should be used as your beginning account balances.)*
- *Exhibit TN 3.3:* This exhibit will be made available by the instructor to students who are ***not*** completing ***Case 3-4***. See footnote 3 (on the next page) for more details.

Requirements:

Dr. Haines asks that you make all adjustments that are necessary in order to produce proper accrual basis financial statements.[1] Specifically, you are to complete the following.

1. Determine which 12/31/10 account balances (*Exhibit TN 3.2*) require adjustment and prepare the required adjusting journal entries.[2]

2. Post the adjusting journal entries from requirement (1) to "T" accounts and calculate the overall account balances.

3. Use the ending balances in the "T" accounts from requirement (2) to prepare a 12/31/10 adjusted trial balance for Dr. Haines' orthodontic practice.[3] Please provide a breakdown of the items being included in "miscellaneous expense."

4. Consider the information you obtained about the two Visa gift cards from your phone call with Dr. Haines on January 3 (*Exhibit 3.5*). Using the accounts listed in *Exhibit TN 3.2*, provide at least two possible alternatives for the debit portion of the resulting journal entry(ies) and explain how the economic entity assumption impacts your choices. Given your two options, please clarify what additional information you would need from Dr. Haines to determine which specific classification best captures the economic reality of this situation.

5. As of 1/1/10, the orthodontic practice reported $6,780 of prepaid insurance as a current asset on its balance sheet. Remember that the prepaid insurance account balance is made up of two separate policies: a 12-month malpractice policy and an 18-month general business liability (GBP) policy. ***Case 3-2*** included entries to record the payments made on 12/21/10 (*Exhibit 3.2*) to renew both policies. Further, it is noted that before this renewal, the last premium payment made towards the general business liability policy took place in June of 2009,

[1] After considering the information provided in the accompanying exhibits, determine whether there are any *additional* adjustments that need to be made in order to produce proper accrual basis financial statements. Start by going through the unadjusted trial balance in *Exhibit TN 3.2* and for each account balance ask yourself, "Is this a deferred revenue or expense?" If so, then determine whether the account balance requires adjustment as of 12/31/10. For each of the remaining accounts, then ask yourself, "Is there any accrued revenue or accrued expense related to this account that still needs to be recorded?"

[2] Please use the account titles listed in *Exhibit TN 3.2* for purposes of your entries. If you need to create a new account, please do so, but clearly label it as to its type (asset, liability, equity, revenue, or expense). You may also find it helpful to review the detailed descriptions of the 11/30 account balances contained in *Exhibit 3.1*.

[3] If you are required to complete ***Case 3-4***, you will prepare additional adjusting entries as a result of the information provided in that case, and your adjusted trial balance will accordingly not be finalized until after these additional entries. If you are not required to complete ***Case 3-4***, you should receive *Exhibit TN 3.3* from your instructor; it will provide you with the necessary information to prepare all adjusting entries as well as your final adjusted trial balance.

totaling $5,670 (the effective date of this policy was 7/1/09). Given this information as well as the information provided in the ***Narrative***, prepare the following:

a. Complete the following analysis for the insurance expense account:

	Insurance Expense Recorded		
	1/1 to 11/30	12/1-12/31	Total
Malpractice	?	?	?
General Business (GBP) Liability	?	?	?
Total Insurance Expense	?[4]	?	?

b. Complete the following analysis for the prepaid insurance account:

	Malpractice	**GBP**	**Total**
Prepaid insurance as of 1/1/10	?	?	$6,780.00[5]
Insurance coverage renewals (1/1/10 to 11/30/10)	?	?	?
Insurance coverage expired (1/1/10 to 11/30/10)	(?)	(?)	(?)[6]
Prepaid insurance balance as of 11/30/2010	?	?	?[6]
Insurance coverage renewals (12/1/10 to 12/31/10)	?	?	?
Insurance coverage expired (12/1/10 to 12/31/10)	(?)	(?)	(?)
Prepaid insurance balance as of 12/31/10	?	?	?

You should assume that all insurance policies have been renewed at the end of the policy term. Further, in order to earn any credit, you must show all work.

6. On Saturday, January 8, 2011, the 2010 Depreciation Schedule was received from the outside accounting firm (*Exhibit 3.9b*). Compare *Exhibit 3.9b* to the relevant balances reported on your adjusted trial balance (final answer for requirement (3)). Consider the noted differences. What information (if any) should be communicated to the outside accounting firm about the accuracy of this schedule? Why is this communication important? Explain.

---

[4] You are encouraged to utilize the relevant balances reported in *Exhibit 3.1* as check figures.

[5] Given the information provided in the ***Narrative*** and *Exhibit 3.2* (12/15 (iii) meetings and 12/21 (iii) insurance renewal), calculate the portion of each policy that should have still been prepaid at 1/1/2010. Roll the account balance forward to 11/30 and then again to 12/31 using the template provided here.

[6] You are encouraged to utilize the relevant balances reported in *Exhibit 3.1* as check figures.

Case 3-4

Preparing the Bank Reconciliation

Your winter break has gone by quickly since graduating with your accounting degree in early December. While you planned to relax before beginning your career with a national public accounting firm, instead you found yourself assisting family friend Dr. Tamera Haines by preparing financial statements for her orthodontic practice. To date, you have assisted Dr. Haines by recording her practice's December transactions and adjusting entries.

You initially assumed that the outside accounting firm would prepare the December bank reconciliation. Dr. Haines explained that although the reconciliation is typically prepared by the outside accountants, her office manager Paddy is the one who provides them with all the necessary information. Paddy also reviews (per her request) the reconciliation for accuracy when it is received back from the accountants. With Paddy still out of town and the 2010 financial statements not yet finished, Dr. Haines asks if you might be willing to help expedite the process by preparing the December bank reconciliation yourself. You agree to help, and after rummaging around Paddy's office, you locate the following:

- *Exhibit 3.11*: The November bank reconciliation (prepared by the outside accounting firm).
- *Exhibit 3.12a*: The December bank statement received in the mail in early January (prepared by the bank).
- *Exhibit 3.12b*: Details of items noted in the December bank statement.
- *Exhibit TN 3.4*: The checkbook maintained by Paddy through the end of December and updated by you for the checks written in January, as well as the December deposit tickets.[1]
- *Exhibit TN 3.5*: Details of the general ledger cash balance reported in *Exhibit TN 3.6* (needed for requirement (2) only— ***available from your instructor***).

[1] Note that bank deposits made after 4:00 p.m. are not credited to the account by the bank until the following business day.

- *Exhibit TN 3.6*: The 12/31/2010 account balances that include all necessary adjusting entries *except* those additional entries that will be recorded in this case ***(available from your instructor)***.

Requirements:

1. Prepare the December bank reconciliation, reconciling the checkbook provided in *Exhibit TN 3.4* to the bank statement provided in *Exhibit 3.12a*. A reconciliation template has been provided for your use on the subsequent pages. Be sure to clearly explain all reconciling items, and when determining the nature of certain reconciling items, please note that the bank *has not* made any errors in reporting the December activity.
2. Please complete the following:
   a. Compare the final reconciled checkbook balance (that is, the final answer from requirement (1)) to the cash balance reported on the general ledger (*Exhibits TN 3.5* and *TN 3.6*), and explain all differences (if any).
   b. Prepare all adjusting entries that are necessary as a result of the bank reconciliation process.[2]
   c. Consider whether there is anything else that should be brought to management's attention as a result of your findings from reconciling the cash account. If so, explain.

[2] Please provide a thorough description of all proposed entries and use the account titles listed in *Exhibit TN 3.6* for purposes of your entries. If you need to create a new account, please do so, but clearly label it as to its type (asset, liability, equity, revenue, or expense).

Bank Balance per 12/31 Bank Statement $ 395,394.74

Plus: Deposits in Transit (list individually)

Errors and other items (list individually and explain):

Explanation

Less: Outstanding Checks (list individually)

Errors and other items (list individually and explain):

Explanation

Reconciled Balance per Bank at 12/31 $

Unadjusted Balance per Checkbook at 12/31 $ (5,812.43)

Plus: Interest earned during December ______________

Errors and other items (list individually and explain):

Explanation

______________________________ ______________

______________________________ ______________

______________________________ ______________

______________________________ ______________

Less: Bank Service Fee ______________

Errors and other items (list individually and explain):

Explanation

______________________________ ______________

______________________________ ______________

______________________________ ______________

______________________________ ______________

Reconciled Balance per Checkbook at 12/31 $______________

Case 3-5

Preparing the Financial Statements

With just a few weeks left before your move to Chicago to begin your career with a national public accounting firm, you find that you are almost done assisting your family friend Dr. Tamera Haines. You have enjoyed being able to help her while Paddy, her office manager, has been out on vacation. While you never anticipated spending your entire break working, your experience has been a rewarding one, and Dr. Haines is very grateful to you for your efforts. You are now ready to prepare her practice's December 31, 2010 financial statements and have been provided with the following item in order to assist you with this task.

- *Exhibit TN 3.7*: The final 12/31/2010 account balances after all adjusting entries ***(available from your instructor)***.

Requirements:

1. Using good form, prepare the following December 31, 2010 financial statements:[1]
    a. The Balance Sheet.
    b. The Income Statement (for the 12 months ended).
    c. The Statement of Shareholder's Equity (for the 12 months ended).[2]
2. Prepare all necessary closing entries.
3. Prepare a post-closing trial balance *(in good form)*.

[1] In order to determine the proper classification of the account balances included in *Exhibit TN 3.7*, you are encouraged to review the ***Narrative*** and, if necessary, information provided in *Exhibits 3.1-3.12b*.
[2] Please note that Dr. Haines has not made any additional capital contributions during the year.

Case 3-6

Analyzing Cash Flows

As you count down your last few days of freedom before you begin your new accounting position in Chicago, you drop by the orthodontic practice of Dr. Tamera Haines, your family friend, to say goodbye. Happy that you visited, Dr. Haines steps away for a moment from one of her patients to greet you. She expresses her gratitude to you for assisting her with the preparation of her practice's financial statements during the absence of her office manager Paddy, especially since you were supposed to be on break after recently graduating. She then asks (with a smile on her face) if you would have time to assist her with one last task before you go. Specifically, Dr. Haines asks if you would prepare an analysis of her practice's cash flow during 2010. The accountants have asked for this analysis and will utilize it when preparing the last remaining financial statement for 2010, the Statement of Cash Flows. Still very appreciative of the generous bonus she paid you at the end of your brief employment and mindful of the cost of living in Chicago, you agree to help.

To prepare for this analysis, you were able to gather the following items (***to be provided by your instructor***):

- *Exhibit TN 3.8a*: A Comparative 12/31 Balance Sheet for 2009 and 2010.
- *Exhibit TN 3.8b*: The Income Statement for the 12 months ended 12/31/2010.
- *Exhibit TN 3.8c*: The Statement of Equity for the 12 months ended 12/31/2010.
- *Exhibit TN 3.9*: Additional Information.
- *Exhibit TN 3.10*: Sources and Uses of Cash Schedule (to complete Requirement (7)).

Requirements:

1. Analyze the Accounts Receivable account and calculate the cash collected from patients as payments on account.
2. Analyze the Unearned Patient Treatment Revenue account and calculate the amount of cash collected during 2010 from patients as contract deposits.

3. Analyze the Credit Card Receivable account and calculate the amount of cash automatically deposited to the checking account in 2010 by Care Credit™ (net of the 3% service fee).

4. Analyze the Visa Gift Card account and calculate the amount of cash paid in 2010 for Visa Gift Card purchases.

5. Analyze Inventory of Super Smile, Orthodontic Supplies, and Accounts Payable, and calculate the amount of cash paid during 2010 to vendors for purchases made on account.

6. Analyze the Prepaid Advertising account and calculate the amount of cash paid in 2010 for advertising.

7. Use your answers to the above requirements (1)—(6) to complete the Sources and Uses of Cash Schedule presented in *Exhibit TN 3.10* ***(available from your instructor)***.

Exhibit 3.1: Account Listing

Ref. No.	Account Description		11/30/2010 balance
1	2010 Depreciation (*Exhibit 3.9b*).	$	17,320.63
2	Amount owed to vendor Ortho Technologies.		2,500.00
3	Balance due from Care Credit.™		9,612.91
4	Balance due from patients for services rendered.		409,093.33
5	Capital stock.		25,000.00
6	**Cash in bank (solve for unknown).**		**?**
7	Certificate of deposit owned.		350,000.00
8	Cost of bad debt.		21,750.00
9	Cost of building maintenance.		750.00
10	Cost of charitable donations.		15,680.10
11	Cost of cleaning and laundry services.		2,332.00
12	Cost of credit card service fees.		25,386.73
13	Cost of employee uniform reimbursements.		1,800.00
14	Cost of employer 2010 payroll taxes.		26,279.99
15	Cost of health insurance premiums.		72,600.00
16	Cost of insurance coverage expired.		6,215.00
17	Cost of lab fees.		6,875.00
18	Cost of license and professional certification fees.		1,600.00
19	Cost of miscellaneous items.		1,166.00
20	Cost of monthly rent incurred.		115,500.00
21	Cost of office supplies used.		4,532.00
22	Cost of orthodontic supplies used.		282,243.00
23	Cost of outside accounting services.		1,625.00
24	Cost of patient referral rewards.		2,600.00
25	Cost of patient relations and events.		1,200.00
26	Cost of radio advertising completed in 2010.		26,425.00
27	Cost of repairs.		850.00
28	Cost of salaries incurred.		479,848.20
29	Cost of telephone service.		5,775.00
30	Cost of training and professional education.		13,600.00
31	Cost of utilities.		4,580.00
32	Cumulative depreciation on furniture, fixtures & equip. (*Exhibit 3.9b*)		63,606.51
33	Dividends paid to owner in 2010.		125,000.00
34	Furniture, fixtures and equipment owned (*Exhibit 3.9b*).		161,870.00
35	Insurance coverage owned but not yet used.		565.00
36	Office supplies owned.		925.00
37	Orthodontic supplies owned.		49,808.00
38	Patient contract advances collected.		440,771.16
39	Patient late fees earned.		550.00
40	Patient treatment revenue earned.		1,568,009.67
41	Petty cash (monitored by Carol).		100.00
42	Radio advertisements purchased not yet used.		850.00
43	Retained earnings, January 1, 2010.		232,273.98
44	Super Smile sales revenue.		7,700.00
45	Super Smile whitening systems owned (*Exhibit 3.6*).		10,035.13
46	Visa gift cards owned.		1,400.00

Exhibit 3.2: Paddy's December 2010 Notes

Wednesday, December 1:

i. Emailed the December patient monthly billing, which totaled $62,345.
ii. Leslie's birthday! Ordered lunch for the staff from Jimmy John's. Paid $62 (check #653).
iii. Called Mr. Knox about his delinquent account balance.

Friday, December 3:

i. Interviewed two job candidates to stand in for Linda while she is on maternity leave.
ii. Went to Staples and purchased office supplies. Paid $225 (check #655). Voided check #654.
iii. Met with Mrs. Lienhart and stopped by Cole Jackson's house to pick up a payment (*Exhibit 3.4*).
iv. Dr. Haines was interviewed by the local newspaper. The interview will run on January 2, 2011 in a special weekend supplement focusing on health and wellness. After the interview, I met with the sales manager and arranged to purchase some advertising in the issue.
v. Paid a copy machine repairman to fix the copier. Paid $400 (check #656).

Saturday, December 4:

i. Met with Lisa Jenks about her family's relocation to Tampa and had her sign termination papers. Refunded the Jenks family their deposit totaling $845 (check #657).
ii. Reimbursed Leslie $110 for uniform purchases (check #658).
iii. Mr. Helm (our landlord) stopped by for a follow up to his initial treatment consultation. He proposed that instead of paying him December's rent ($10,500), we instead provide his extensive orthodontic services "for free."[1] Dr. Haines accepted his offer but made it clear to me privately that we will still book the revenue as "she doesn't want anyone to ever be able to accuse her of tax evasion."

Tuesday, December 7:

i. Met with a Xerox representative to discuss buying a new copy machine.
ii. Met with Karen Little about her outstanding account balance. Drove to her house and picked up a payment (*Exhibit 3.4*).
iii. Handed out four referral fee awards! Two patients chose gift certificates (and used them today) and two patients chose Visa gift cards.
iv. Purchased letterhead and business cards with the business name, logo, and address on account. Vendor: Precision Graphics, list price $550. Payment terms of 1/10, n/30.

[1] Mr. Helm did not benefit at a young age from an interceptive treatment plan. As such, his treatment plan is more extensive and is expected to last 30 months.

Shipment (FOB shipping point) has been promised to take place no later than December 12.[2]

Thursday, December 9:

i. Electronically registered Dr. Haines for a two-day CPE course that will take place later in the month.
ii. Paid Ambassador's Outdoor Services $450 (#659) for tree trimming and yard cleanup.
iii. Met with Stephen Butler about his family's relocation and had him sign a termination agreement. Refunded the Butler family their two deposits totaling $1,610 (check #660).
iv. Paid the copy machine repairman another $150 for a service call (check #661).
v. Discussed the copy machine purchase with Dr. Haines. She has decided to go with the Work Centre copy machine from LTS Copy Services located just 20 minutes away in Atlanta. The copier chosen has a list price of $11,050 and should be delivered FOB shipping point by the end of the month. Dr. Haines chose to upgrade to "white glove" delivery because it includes both the installation and initial setup.

Saturday, December 11:

i. Received an email that the business cards and letterhead ordered on December 7 have been shipped.
ii. Ordered the copy machine from LTS.
iii. Handed out two referral fee awards: a Visa gift card and a gift certificate (which was immediately used by the patient).
iv. Received the payroll report (*Exhibit 3.3a*). Prepared and distributed paychecks:

Figure 3.2

December 11:	Paycheck #
Lauren Smith	662
Leslie Tomah	663
Linda Williams	664
Carol Plumb	665
Paddy Singleton	666
Tamera Haines	667

Wednesday, December 15:

i. Received and paid the invoice from *Lithia Springs Gazette* for the newspaper ad included in the special health supplement and for some smaller advertisements that ran the first week of the month. Paid $2,650 (check #668), $1600 of which was for the ad in the weekend supplement.

[2] For purposes of the discount, assume that the 10-day period begins at the time of title transfer.

ii. Paid Ortho Technologies $2,500 for our entire outstanding account balance related to orthodontic supplies purchased (and delivered) in November (check #669).
iii. Met with various local insurance agents to get bids on our two insurance policies (12-month malpractice policy and an 18-month general business policy) both of which have policy terms that expire as of 12/31/10.

Friday, December 17:

i. Received an email from Jackie Whitman (certified dental assistant). She has accepted our offer to work during Linda's maternity leave and will start on February 1, 2011.
ii. Business cards and letterhead arrived. We were charged $50 for shipping on top of the $550 for the merchandise! Called and complained but to no avail. Went ahead and paid the invoice (with check #670) in order to get the 1% discount.[3]

Saturday, December 18:

i. Sold two Super Smile Whitening systems for $110 each (*Exhibit 3.4*).
ii. Picked up a check from Micah Davis (*Exhibit 3.4*).
iii. Signed up for 12-month subscriptions of 9 different magazines for the lobby. Purchased from patient Hannah Miller (fundraiser for West Hollow Elementary School). All nine of these 12-month subscriptions are effective immediately. Cost: $165 (check #671).
iv. Counted the petty cash noting that $75 had been used since December 1.
    a. $32 for dry cleaning Dr. Haines' lab coats.
    b. $28 uniform reimbursement to Lauren.
    c. $15 for Girl Scout cookies bought from Anna Wilson and shared with the staff.
v. Cashed a check (#672) for $75 and used it to replenish the petty cash drawer.

Tuesday, December 21:

i. Ordered a large amount of orthodontic supplies (brackets, bands, and wires). Vendor: Ortho Technologies, list price $16,500. Negotiated a trade discount of 5% and payment terms of 2/10, n/30. Shipment (FOB destination) has been promised to take place no later than December 26.
ii. Met with Valerie Cregg to discuss her outstanding account balance. She concluded that she should delay treatment for her youngest child until treatment is finished for the older child. She signed a termination agreement and gave me permission to apply her younger child's deposit of $915 toward her older child's outstanding account balance.
iii. Went ahead and renewed the two insurance policies expiring 12/31/10. New malpractice policy is $3,300 for 12 months, and new business insurance policy is $6,210 for 18 months. Both policies are effective 1/1/2011. Premiums were paid in full (check #673).
iv. Paid $3,250 (check #674) to sponsor two little league teams. The team jerseys will have the office name and logo. The season starts in May and finishes at the end of June.

---

[3] For purposes of the discount, assume that the 10-day period begins at the time of title transfer, and the discount applies to the merchandise only (and not the shipping charge).

Wednesday, December 22:

i. The office is closed starting tomorrow until we re-open on Tuesday, December 28.[4] Received the payroll data early (*Exhibit 3.3b*), prepared the checks, and distributed them before the holiday. The checks are dated 12/25/10.

Figure 3.3

December 25:	Paycheck #
Lauren Smith	675
Leslie Tomah	676
Linda Williams	677
Carol Plumb	678
Paddy Singleton	679
Tamera Haines	680

ii. Paid the accounting firm $160 for their December services (check # 681).
iii. Dr. Haines surprised the entire staff by letting each of us have one of the $100 Visa gift cards!
iv. Wrote the following checks to local charities:

Lithia Springs High School Booster Club	$1,500	(#682)
Art for Kidz	$ 150	(#683)
Lithia Springs Youth Recreation Club	$1,500	(#684)
PTA Georgia Congress	$ 350	(#685)

v. Sold three more Super Smile Whitening systems as last-minute holiday gifts! This brings us to 75 units sold in total for the year (*Exhibit 3.4*).

Wednesday, December 29:

i. Met with David Adams about his account balance and determined that $2,250 of receivables should be written off as uncollectible.[5]
ii. Paid Dr. Haines a quarterly dividend check totaling $60,000 (check #686).
iii. Purchased ten more Visa gift cards, $1,000 (check #687).
iv. Submitted payment for the entire amount of December employee payroll withholdings to the appropriate taxing authority (check #688).
v. Paid our December payroll taxes (i.e., employer's share of the FICA tax) to the appropriate taxing authority (check #689).
vi. Received a courtesy call from LTS Copier services to schedule delivery. The copy machine is scheduled to leave its facility in Atlanta between 10:00 a.m. and 11:00 a.m. on

[4] Assume the staff is paid for all holidays that fall during the work week.
[5] Assume that the company uses the "direct write-off" method when accounting for bad debt. Under this method, bad debt expense is recorded at the time the patient receivable is written off.

Friday. Someone from our office has to be present in order to sign and accept the delivery. Setup and training should take no more than 45 minutes.

Friday, December 31:

i. The new copy machine was delivered. Even though it works fine, disappointingly, it has a very noticeable dent. Our Xerox service representative lowered the price $250 and did not charge us for the "white glove" delivery. I charged the balance due on the corporate credit card.

ii. The office is closed New Year's Day.

Exhibit 3.3a: December 11 Payroll Records

December 11:	Annual Salary	Gross Pay	FICA W/H[6]	FIT W/H	SIT W/H	Net Pay
Lauren Smith	$ 37,200.00	$ 1,550.00	$118.58	$ 124.00	$ 46.50	$ 1,260.92
Leslie Tomah	49,200.00	2,050.00	156.83	225.50	61.50	1,606.17
Linda Williams	52,800.00	2,200.00	168.30	308.00	66.00	1,657.70
Carol Plumb	24,480.00	1,020.00	78.03	142.80	30.60	768.57
Paddy Singleton	72,000.00	3,000.00	229.50	420.00	90.00	2,260.50
Tamera Haines	300,000.00	12,500.00	181.25	3,125.00	375.00	8,818.75
Total	**$535,680.00**	**$22,320.00**	**$932.49**	**$4,345.30**	**$669.60**	**$16,372.61**

Exhibit 3.3b: December 25 Payroll Records

December 25:	Annual Salary	Gross Pay	FICA W/H	FIT W/H	SIT W/H	Net Pay
Lauren Smith	$ 37,200.00	$ 1,550.00	$118.58	$ 124.00	$ 46.50	$ 1,260.92
Leslie Tomah	49,200.00	2,050.00	156.83	225.50	61.50	1,606.17
Linda Williams	52,800.00	2,200.00	168.30	308.00	66.00	1,657.70
Carol Plumb	24,480.00	1,020.00	78.03	142.80	30.60	768.57
Paddy Singleton	72,000.00	3,000.00	229.50	420.00	90.00	2,260.50
Tamera Haines	300,000.00	12,500.00	181.25	3,125.00	375.00	8,818.75
Total	**$535,680.00**	**$22,320.00**	**$932.49**	**$4,345.30**	**$669.60**	**$16,372.61**

[6] FICA, Federal Income Tax (FIT), State Income Tax (SIT) are all taxes being paid by the employee. The government requires the employer to withhold the amount owed by the employee directly from the employees' pay checks. The employer is then obligated to submit the money withheld (on the employees' behalves) directly to the taxing authority. In addition, the employer also has to pay FICA tax. In 2010, the employer's FICA tax was the same dollar amount as the employees' FICA tax, and it is considered an additional paid out-of-pocket expense of the employer. In this case, the total FICA amount being withheld (per payroll period) on the behalf of the employees is $932.49. When adding the equivalent amount of $932.49 to be paid by the *employer*, this results in a total FICA tax of $1,864.98 being paid to the government (per payroll period) by Haines' orthodontics practice.

Exhibit 3.4: December 2010 Daily Collections Summary

	Payments on Account			New Patient Deposits			Super Smile Sales			Grand Total		
Date	Cash	Credit Card	Total	Cash	Credit Card	Total	Cash	Credit Card	Total	Cash	Credit Card	Total
Wed., December 1	$ 2,329.67	$ 998.43	$3,328.10							$2,329.67	$998.43	$3,328.10
Thurs., December 2	2,633.09	1,755.39	4,388.48	$ 833.00		$ 833.00				3,466.09	1,755.39	5,221.48
Fri., December 3	1,690.24	724.39	2,414.63		$1,062.50	1,062.50				1,690.24	1,786.89	3,477.13
Sat., December 4	574.91	1,341.46	1,916.37							574.91	1,341.46	1,916.37
Tues., December 7	3,577.22	1,533.10	5,110.32	799.00	748.00	1,547.00				4,376.22	2,281.10	6,657.32
Wed., December 8	2,069.68	804.88	2,874.56	1,615.00		1,615.00				3,684.68	804.88	4,489.56
Thurs., December 9	1,993.02	1,839.72	3,832.74		782.00	782.00				1,993.02	2,621.72	4,614.74
Fri., December 10	1,360.62	3,174.79	4,535.41							1,360.62	3,174.79	4,535.41
Sat., December 11	3,577.22	1,533.10	5,110.32							3,577.22	1,533.10	5,110.32
Tues., December, 14	3,315.32	2,210.21	5,525.53	977.50	994.50	1,972.00				4,292.82	3,204.71	7,497.53
Wed., December 15	1,425.78	554.47	1,980.25							1,425.78	554.47	1,980.25
Thurs., December 16	383.27	894.31	1,277.58	1,657.50	918.00	2,575.50				2,040.77	1,812.31	3,853.08
Fri., December 17	2,459.34	1,054.00	3,513.34							2,459.34	1,054.00	3,513.34
Sat., December 18	1,609.75	626.01	2,235.76	663.00	837.95	1,500.95	$220.00		$220.00	2,492.75	1,463.96	3,956.71
Tues., December 21	1,842.27	789.54	2,631.81							1,842.27	789.54	2,631.81
Wed., December 22	1,962.36	1,308.24	3,270.60		833.00	833.00	330.00		330.00	2,292.36	2,141.24	4,433.60
Tues., December 28	1,945.12	833.62	2,778.74	869.55	756.50	1,626.05				2,814.67	1,590.12	4,404.79
Wed., December 29	2,391.63	930.08	3,321.71	782.00		782.00				3,173.63	930.08	4,103.71
Thurs., December 30	408.19	952.44	1,360.63							408.19	952.44	*1,360.63
Fri., December 31	1,285.50	1,186.62	2,472.12							1,285.50	1,186.62	*2,472.12
	$38,834.20	**$25,044.80**	**$63,879.00**	**$8,196.55**	**$6,932.45**	**$15,129.00**	**$550.00**	**$0.00**	**$550.00**	**$47,580.75**	**$31,977.25**	**$79,558.00**

*Deposited on Friday, December 31.

Exhibit 3.5: Summary of January 2011 Events

Monday, January 3:

You go to the office bright and early in order to meet Carol and assist her (with Dr. Haines' permission) in counting supplies and other verifiable assets. After a long morning of counting, you determine the following:

i. Roughly 5 percent of the business cards and letterhead purchased in December had been used (*Exhibit 3.2*, 12/7(iv), 12/11(i), and 12/17(ii)). Of the remaining office supplies, roughly $175 worth was counted as still on hand.
ii. $26,000 of orthodontic supplies was on hand.
iii. $100 Visa Gift Cards; 14 were on hand.
iv. Petty Cash totaling $12 was counted. The Petty Cash drawer contained the following three receipts:
    a. Boy Scout Popcorn purchased from patient Joey Howard and shared with the staff: $18.
    b. Dry Cleaning receipts: $52.
    c. USPS for postage: $14.
v. 37 Super Smile Whitening Systems were on hand. Carol rummaged around in Paddy's office and was able to locate a summary schedule detailing all of the Super Smile purchases for the year (*Exhibit 3.6*).

After a quick phone call to Dr. Haines, it was decided to treat the oldest Super Smile units on hand as being sold first and to write off any petty cash shortfall to "Miscellaneous Expense." Dr. Haines also shared that on the previous Friday she had taken with her two of the Visa gift cards so that she could use them as gifts during her family gift exchange.

Upon arriving back at the office after lunch, you and Carol noticed that two deliveries had been made while you were away. Specifically, the two deliveries were:

vi. The 12/21/2010 Ortho Technologies order (*Exhibit 3.2*).
vii. A shipment of 50 Super Smile Whitening Systems. The box included an invoice (*Exhibit 3.7*) and a packing slip showing a shipping time and date of 12:00 p.m. on 12/30/2010.

Before calling it a day, you helped Carol unpack and put away both deliveries.

Tuesday, January 4:

i. With Carol's assistance, you emailed the January patient monthly billing that totaled $57,585. With a little fiddling, you were able to better understand the billing software and determined that $16,850 and $17,210 of patient services were performed for patients who were in their last three months of treatment in December and January, respectfully. The system does not generate bills for these patients as they were already required to pay for their final three months of treatment in advance.[7]

ii. At Dr. Haines request, you began making the Wednesday and Saturday bank deposits (*Exhibit 3.8*).

iii. You mailed the January health insurance premium payment totaling $6,850 (check #690).

iv. The local evening news television program interviewed Dr. Haines as a follow-up to the story that ran over the weekend in the special health supplement. Five new patient consultations were booked as a result of the ad that ran in the supplement.

Wednesday, January 5:

i. The local radio station called and explained that all of the advertising credits existing at 11/30/10 had been fully utilized as a result of the radio advertisements that ran in December. The station manager informed you that he needed another check by 5:00 p.m. today in order for the radio ad campaign to continue without interruption. After discussing this with Dr. Haines, you hand-delivered a $2,400 check to the radio station (check #691).

ii. You and Carol together met with Nancy Jaine about her family's upcoming relocation to Toronto. It was decided to apply the Jaine family contract deposit toward their outstanding account balance. In addition to applying the deposit, Mrs. Jaine paid the remaining balance due of $1,050 (*Exhibit 3.8*).

iii. As another result of the weekend article and interview, a local elementary school invited Dr. Haines to speak at its career day. In addition to business cards, Dr. Haines handed out $225 worth of toothbrushes and toothpaste to the students (orthodontic supplies).

iv. Dr. Haines prepared a check (#692) for $88 cash and asked you to cash it during your regular Wednesday trip to the bank. You did so and put the cash in the Petty Cash drawer on Thursday morning.

Saturday, January 8:

You received both the payroll report and the year-end depreciation schedule from the outside accounting firm (*Exhibits 3.9a & 3.9b*). You prepared the payroll checks and gave them to Dr. Haines to sign and distribute.

Figure 3.4

January 8:	Paycheck #
Lauren Smith	693
Leslie Tomah	694
Linda Williams	695
Carol Plumb	696
Paddy Singleton	697
Tamera Haines	698

[7] Other than the December advance payment received by landlord Mr. Helm (*Exhibit 3.2*, 12/4(iii)), the account "Unearned Patient Treatment Revenue" is used only for recording the deposits received from patients in advance for their last three months of services. You should assume that Paddy has already adjusted this account for deposits earned during January through November of 2010.

Tuesday, January 11:

i. You went through the mail, preparing the following checks that were signed and mailed by Dr. Haines:
   a. The $424 utility bill for December (#699).
   b. The $185 phone bill for December (#700).
   c. The December corporate credit card bill was paid in full (#701) (see *Exhibit 3.10*).

ii. In addition, you prepared payments as follows:
   a. For the Orthodontic supplies received on 1/3/10 (#702).
   b. For January rent of $10,500 (#703).

Dr. Haines signed the checks and the payments were mailed.

Friday, January 14:

The December bank statement was received in the mail.

- Students who will not be required to complete ***Case 3-4*** should incorporate *Exhibit TN 3.3* here and prepare all entries that should be made as a result of the information provided in this exhibit.
- Students who will be required to complete ***Case 3-4*** should move on with the problem. All entries that should be made as a result of reconciling the December bank statement will be recorded in ***Case 3-4***.

Exhibit 3.6: Super Smile 2010 Inventory Purchases

	# Units	*Average Unit Price Paid	Total Price Paid
1/1 Beginning Inventory	16	$86.600	$ 1,385.60
2/1 Purchases	24	$87.972	2,111.33
4/1 Purchases	24	$89.371	2,144.90
7/1 Purchases	24	$90.799	2,179.18
10/1 Purchases	24	$92.255	2,214.12
Total	**112**		**$10,035.13**

Summary:	#	$
1/1 Beginning Inventory	16	$1,385.60
2010 Purchases	96	8,649.53
Total Units Available	**112**	**$10,035.13**

*This represents the average unit price paid after taking into account all costs of acquiring the units (that is, shipping charges, sales tax, and purchase discounts).

Note for students completing ***Case 3-3***: Compare *Exhibit 3.6* to the relevant balances reported on your unadjusted trial balance (*Exhibit TN 3.2*), and consider if the account balances require adjustments before they are reported on the 12/31/10 financial statements.

Exhibit 3.7: Super Smile Whitening Systems Invoice

Super Smile, Inc

Professional Teeth Whitening & Oral Care Products

INVOICE

123 #3rd Avenue
New York, New York 10003
Phone 1-800-999-2415 Fax 1-800-999-2416

INVOICE #7956
DATE: 12/29/2010

TO:
Dr. Tamera Haines
Haines Professional Orthodontic Practice
3645 Market Place Blvd
Suite 1A & B
Lithia Springs, GA 30344

FOR:
50 Whitening Systems

TERMS:
FOB Shipping Point
1/10, n/30

DESCRIPTION	AMOUNT
50 Consumer Whitening Systems	$4,300.00
Sales Tax	172.00
Shipping and insurance	125.00
TOTAL	**$4,597.00**

Make all checks payable to Super Smile, Inc.

Thank you for your business!

Exhibit 3.8: January 2011 Daily Collections Summary (1st two weeks)

	Payments on Account			New Patient Deposits			Super Smile Sales			Grand Total		
Date	Cash	Credit Card	Total	Cash	Credit Card	Total	Cash	Credit Card	Total	Cash	Credit	Card
Tues., Jan. 4	$1,780.30	$ 961.36	$2,741.66							$ 1,780.30	$ 961.36	$ 2,741.66
Wed., Jan.5	2,336.73	1,261.83	3,598.56		$1,681.00	$1,681.00		$220.00	$220.00	2,336.73	3,162.83	5,499.56
Thurs., Jan. 6	1,923.34	1,038.60	2,961.94							1,923.34	1,038.60	2,961.94
Fri., Jan. 7	1,996.92	1,078.33	3,075.25	$ 882.53	831.25	1,713.78				2,879.45	1,909.58	4,789.03
Sat., Jan. 8	2,407.58	1,300.09	$3,707.67							2,407.58	1,300.09	3,707.67
Tues., Jan. 11	2,005.94	1,083.21	3,089.15	1,037.60	811.74	1,849.34				3,043.54	1,894.95	4,938.49
Wed., Jan. 12	2,333.12	1,259.89	3,593.01	747.88	1,317.74	2,065.62	$110.00	110.00	220.00	3,191.00	2,687.63	5,878.63
Thurs., Jan. 13	2,329.51	1,257.94	3,587.45							2,329.51	1,257.94	3,587.45
Fri., Jan. 14	2,206.31	1,191.41	3,397.72	1,260.75	839.46	2,100.21				3,467.06	2,030.87	5,497.93
Sat., Jan. 15	2,199.99	1,188.00	3,387.99							2,199.99	1,188.00	3,387.99
	$21,519.74	**$11,620.66**	**$33,140.40**	**$3,928.76**	**$5,481.19**	**$9,409.95**	**$110.00**	**$330.00**	**$440.00**	**$25,558.50**	**$17,431.85**	**$42,990.35**

Exhibit 3.9a: January 2011 Payroll Records [8]

January 8:	Annual Salary	Gross Pay	FICA W/H	FIT W/H	SIT W/H	Net Pay
Lauren Smith	$ 37,200.00	$ 1,550.00	$ 118.58	$ 124.00	$ 46.50	$ 1,260.92
Leslie Tomah	49,200.00	2,050.00	156.83	225.50	61.50	1,606.17
Linda Williams	52,800.00	2,200.00	168.30	308.00	66.00	1,657.70
Carol Plumb	24,480.00	1,020.00	78.03	142.80	30.60	768.57
Paddy Singleton	72,000.00	3,000.00	229.50	420.00	90.00	2,260.50
Tamera Haines	300,000.00	12,500.00	956.25	3,125.00	375.00	8,043.75
Total	**$535,680.00**	**$22,320.00**	**$1,707.49**	**$4,345.30**	**$669.60**	**$15,597.61**

Exhibit 3.9b: 2010 Depreciation Schedule

Equipment	Cost	Date Purch.	Life*	Monthly Dep.	A/D 12/31/09	Jan.-Nov. 2010	A/D 11/30/10	Dec. 2010	A/D 12/31/10
Dental Chairs	$7,470.00	1/1/05	5		$7,470.00	-	$7,470.00	-	$7,470.00
Waiting Room	12,000.00	1/1/05	5		12,000.00	-	12,000.00	-	12,000.00
Copy Machine	7,200.00	1/1/05	5		7,200.00	-	7,200.00	-	7,200.00
Computers	6,000.00	1/1/08	3	$166.67	4,000.00	$1,833.37	5,833.37	$166.67	6,000.04
Office Furniture	12,800.00	1/1/05	5		12,800.00	-	12,800.00	-	12,800.00
Xray	115,000.00	11/1/09	7	1,369.05	2,738.10	15,059.55	17,797.65	1,369.05	19,166.70
Sterilization Equipment	1,400.00	11/1/09	3	38.89	77.78	427.71	505.49	38.89	544.38
	$161,870.00				$ 46,285.88	$17,320.63	$63,606.51	$1,574.61	$65,181.12

* in years

[8] Per the ***Narrative***, the orthodontic practice is open Tuesday through Saturday. Please consider that employees are paid in the 2nd and 4th Saturday of each month and receive paid holidays (if the holiday lands on a regular work day). Hence, the January 2011 payroll (*Exhibit 3.9a*) began on Tuesday, December 28.

Exhibit 3.10: Corporate Credit Card Summary

Date	Vendor	Amount	Note
12/16/10	Pavilion Dry Cleaners	$ 49.00	
12/17/10	Harmony Dental Lab	325.00	
12/17/10	Delta Airlines	3,000.00	(1)
12/17/10	Disney Resorts	1,375.00	(1)
12/18/10	LLM Professional Education	2,200.00	
12/21/10	T.G.I. Fridays	115.00	(2)
12/23/10	Pavilion Dry Cleaners	65.00	
12/23/10	Harmony Dental Lab	415.00	
12/28/10	Showers of Flowers	45.00	(3)
12/29/10	Office Depot	106.00	(4)
12/31/10	Xerox	10,850.00*	(5)
1/8/11	Pavilion Dry Cleaners	67.00	
1/14/11	Harmony Dental Lab	345.00	
	Total Charges	**$ 18,957.00**	
	Interest Charges	**$ 289.00**	
	Total Amount Owed	**$ 19,246.00**	

Per Conversation with Dr. Haines:

(1) Dr. Haines attended a one-day training course in Orlando on December 18. She flew down on the 12/17 with her husband and two children, flying back on the 12/20. Dr. Haines intends to reimburse the company $3,025 for her family's cost incurred on the trip.

(2) Holiday lunch for the staff.

(3) Flowers sent from the office to Paddy's daughter.

(4) Office supplies purchased by Dr. Haines.

(5) This represents the final purchase price paid for the new copy machine plus an additional $50 hauling fee to remove the old machine (*Exhibit TN 3.2*; *Exhibit 3.2*, 12/9 (v), 12/11(ii), 12/29(vi), and 12/31(i)).

*When reviewing the unadjusted account balances provided in *Exhibit TN 3.2*, it should become apparent that of the above items, only $10,800 (related to the new copy machine), has been recorded.

Exhibit 3.11: The November Bank Reconciliation
(prepared by the outside accounting firm)

Bank Balance per 11/30 Bank Statement	$ **80, 348.80**
Plus: Deposits in Transit (list individually)	
(11/30 deposit)	**2,958.74**
Errors and other items (list individually and explain):	
Explanation	
Less: Outstanding Checks (list individually)	
(#649 Keith Gunning)	**25.00**
(#650 Natalie Edwards)	**26.50**
(#651 Linda Williams)	**48.00**
(#652 Harmony Dental Lab)	**589.74**
Errors and other items (list individually and explain):	
Explanation	
Reconciled Balance per Bank at 11/30	$ **82,618.30**

Exhibit 3.11: The November Bank Reconciliation

(prepared by the outside accounting firm)

Unadjusted Balance per Checkbook at 11/30 $ **47,327.03**

Plus: Interest earned during November ______

Errors and other items (list individually and explain):

Explanation

Explanation	Amount
Care-Credit (November) Direct Deposits	**35,306.27**

Less: Bank Service Fee **15.00**

Errors and other items (list individually and explain):

Explanation

Explanation	Amount

Reconciled Balance per Checkbook at 11/30 $ **82,618.30**

Exhibit 3.12a: The December Bank Statement
(prepared by the bank)

Regions Bank
608 Thornton Road
Lithia Springs, Georgia 30122

Haines Professional Orthodontic Practice
3645 Market Place Blvd Suite 1A & B
Lithia Springs, GA 30344

Account # 2856-95847
Statement Date: 12/31/2010

Balance 12/1/2010	$80,348.80
Checks & Other Debits	118,684.46
Deposits & Other Credits	433,730.40
Balance 12/31/2010	$395,394.74

DATE	**Checks **	
1-Dec	No. 649	25.00
	No. 652	589.74
	No. 653	62.00
4-Dec	No. 655	225.00
	No. 651	48.00
	No. 657	845.00
10-Dec	No. 659	450.00
	No. 660	1,610.00
	No. 656	400.00
13-Dec	No. 662	1,260.92
	No. 663	1,606.17
	No. 664	1,657.70
	No. 665	768.57
	No. 666	2,260.50
	No. 667	8,818.75
20-Dec	No. 668	2,650.00
	No. 669	2,500.00
	No. 661	150.00
	No. 672	75.00
24-Dec	No. 673	9,510.00
	No. 670	594.50
	No. 681	160.00
	No. 682	1,500.00
30-Dec	No. 675	1,620.92
	No. 676	1,606.17
	No. 677	1,657.70
	No. 678	768.57
	No. 679	2,260.50
	No. 680	8,818.75
	No. 683	150.00
	No. 684	1,500.00
	No. 686	60,000.00
	No. 687	1,000.00

	Other Debits	
14-Dec	NSF	1,520.00*
31-Dec	SC	15.00

	Deposits & Other Credits	
1-Dec	DEP	2,958.74
2-Dec	DEP	2,329.67
2-Dec	DD- Care-Credit	11,994.86*
6-Dec	DEP	5,731.24
9-Dec	DEP	8,060.90
13-Dec	DEP	6,930.86
14-Dec	DD- Care-Credit	16,246.19*
16-Dec	DEP	5,718.60
20-Dec	DEP	6,992.86
23-Dec	DEP	4,134.63
24-Dec	DD- Care-Credit	7,581.05*
30-Dec	DEP	3,738.30
31-Dec	CD, INT	351,312.50*

KEY:

SC	Service Charge
OD	Overdraft Charge
DC	Debit Card Purchase
CD	Certificate of Deposit
INT	Interest earned
DD	Direct Deposit
NSF	Insufficient funds

Regions Bank- December 31, 2010 Statement page 1 of 12

*See *Exhibit 3.12b* for more details concerning these items.

#649

Haines Professional Orthodontic Practice
3645 Market Place Blvd Suite 1A and B
Lithia Springs, GA 30344

Date 11/25/2010

Pay to the order of Keith Gunning $ 25.00

Regions Bank
608 Thornton Road, Lithia Springs, GA 30122

Memo: patient relations

Signature: Paddy Singleton

1: 0686748303: 649-2856-95847

#652

Haines Professional Orthodontic Practice
3645 Market Place Blvd Suite 1A and B
Lithia Springs, GA 30344

Date 11/30/2010

Pay to the order of Harmony Dental lab $ 589.74

Regions Bank
608 Thornton Road, Lithia Springs, GA 30122

Memo:

Signature: Paddy Singleton

1: 0686748303: 652-2856-95847

#653

Haines Professional Orthodontic Practice
3645 Market Place Blvd Suite 1A and B
Lithia Springs, GA 30344

Date 12/1/2010

Pay to the order of Jimmy Johns $ 62.00

Regions Bank
608 Thornton Road, Lithia Springs, GA 30122

Memo: Leslie Bday

Signature: Paddy Singleton

1: 0686748303: 653-2856-95847

Regions Bank- December 31, 2010 Statement page 2 of 12

#655

Haines Professional Orthodontic Practice
3645 Market Place Blvd Suite 1A and B
Lithia Springs, GA 30344

Date 12/3/2010

Pay to the order of Staples $ 225.00

Regions Bank
608 Thornton Road, Lithia Springs, GA 30122

Memo:

Signature: Paddy Singleton

1: 0686748303: 655-2856-95847

#651

Haines Professional Orthodontic Practice
3645 Market Place Blvd Suite 1A and B
Lithia Springs, GA 30344

Date 11/30/2010

Pay to the order of Linda Williams $ 48.00

Regions Bank
608 Thornton Road, Lithia Springs, GA 30122

Memo:

Signature: Paddy Singleton

1: 0686748303: 651-2856-95847

#657

Haines Professional Orthodontic Practice
3645 Market Place Blvd Suite 1A and B
Lithia Springs, GA 30344

Date 12/4/2010

Pay to the order of Lisa Jinks $ 845.00

Regions Bank
608 Thornton Road, Lithia Springs, GA 30122

Memo: Contract Deposit

Signature: Paddy Singleton

1: 0686748303: 657-2856-95847

Regions Bank- December 31, 2010 Statement page 3 of 12

#659

Haines Professional Orthodontic Practice
3645 Market Place Blvd Suite 1A and B
Lithia Springs, GA 30344

Date 12/9/2010

Pay to the order of Ambassador Outdoor $ 450.00

Regions Bank
608 Thornton Road, Lithia Springs, GA 30122

Memo:

Signature: Paddy Singleton

1: 0686748303: 659-2856-95847

#660

Haines Professional Orthodontic Practice
3645 Market Place Blvd Suite 1A and B
Lithia Springs, GA 30344

Date 12/9/2010

Pay to the order of Stephen Butler $ 1,610 —

Regions Bank
608 Thornton Road, Lithia Springs, GA 30122

Memo:

Signature: Paddy Singleton

1: 0686748303: 660-2856-95847

#656

Haines Professional Orthodontic Practice
3645 Market Place Blvd Suite 1A and B
Lithia Springs, GA 30344

Date 12/3/2010

Pay to the order of Service Technologies $ 400.00

Regions Bank
608 Thornton Road, Lithia Springs, GA 30122

Memo:

Signature: Paddy Singleton

1: 0686748303: 656-2856-95847

Regions Bank- December 31, 2010 Statement page 4 of 12

#662

Haines Professional Orthodontic Practice
3645 Market Place Blvd Suite 1A and B
Lithia Springs, GA 30344

Date 12/11/2010

Pay to the order of Lauren Smith $ 1,260.92

Regions Bank
608 Thornton Road, Lithia Springs, GA 30122

Memo:

Signature: Paddy Singleton

1: 0686748303: 662-2856-95847

#663

Haines Professional Orthodontic Practice
3645 Market Place Blvd Suite 1A and B
Lithia Springs, GA 30344

Date 12/11/2010

Pay to the order of Leslie Tomah $ 1,606.17

Regions Bank
608 Thornton Road, Lithia Springs, GA 30122

Memo:

Signature: Paddy Singleton

1: 0686748303: 663-2856-95847

#664

Haines Professional Orthodontic Practice
3645 Market Place Blvd Suite 1A and B
Lithia Springs, GA 30344

Date 12/11/2010

Pay to the order of Linda Williams $ 1,657.70

Regions Bank
608 Thornton Road, Lithia Springs, GA 30122

Memo:

Signature: Paddy Singleton

1: 0686748303: 664-2856-95847

Regions Bank- December 31, 2010 Statement page 5 of 12

#665

Haines Professional Orthodontic Practice
3645 Market Place Blvd Suite 1A and B
Lithia Springs, GA 30344

Date 12/11/2010

Pay to the order of Carol Plunk $ 768.57

Regions Bank
608 Thornton Road, Lithia Springs, GA 30122

Memo:

Signature: Paddy Singleton

1: 0686748303: 665-2856-95847

#666

Haines Professional Orthodontic Practice
3645 Market Place Blvd Suite 1A and B
Lithia Springs, GA 30344

Date 12/11/2010

Pay to the order of Paddy Singleton $ 2,260.50

Regions Bank
608 Thornton Road, Lithia Springs, GA 30122

Memo:

Signature: Paddy Singleton

1: 0686748303: 666-2856-95847

#667

Haines Professional Orthodontic Practice
3645 Market Place Blvd Suite 1A and B
Lithia Springs, GA 30344

Date 12/11/2010

Pay to the order of Tamera Haines $ 8,818.75

Regions Bank
608 Thornton Road, Lithia Springs, GA 30122

Memo:

Signature: Paddy Singleton

1: 0686748303: 667-2856-95847

Regions Bank- December 31, 2010 Statement page 6 of 12

#668

Haines Professional Orthodontic Practice
3645 Market Place Blvd Suite 1A and B
Lithia Springs, GA 30344

Date 12/15/2010

Pay to the order of Lithia Springs Gazette $ 2650 —

Regions Bank
608 Thornton Road, Lithia Springs, GA 30122

Memo:

Signature: Paddy Singleton

1: 0686748303: 668-2856-95847

#669

Haines Professional Orthodontic Practice
3645 Market Place Blvd Suite 1A and B
Lithia Springs, GA 30344

Date 12/15/2010

Pay to the order of Ortho Technologies $ 2,500 —

Regions Bank
608 Thornton Road, Lithia Springs, GA 30122

Memo:

Signature: Paddy Singleton

1: 0686748303: 669-2856-95847

#661

Haines Professional Orthodontic Practice
3645 Market Place Blvd Suite 1A and B
Lithia Springs, GA 30344

Date 12/9/2010

Pay to the order of Service Technologies $ 150 00

Regions Bank
608 Thornton Road, Lithia Springs, GA 30122

Memo:

Signature: Paddy Singleton

1: 0686748303: 661-2856-95847

Regions Bank- December 31, 2010 Statement page 7 of 12

#672

Haines Professional Orthodontic Practice
3645 Market Place Blvd Suite 1A and B
Lithia Springs, GA 30344

Date 12/18/2010

Pay to the order of Cash $ 75.00

Regions Bank
608 Thornton Road, Lithia Springs, GA 30122

Memo:

Signature: Paddy Singleton

1: 0686748303: 672-2856-95847

#673

Haines Professional Orthodontic Practice
3645 Market Place Blvd Suite 1A and B
Lithia Springs, GA 30344

Date 12/21/2010

Pay to the order of Nationwide Insurance $ 9,510 –

Regions Bank
608 Thornton Road, Lithia Springs, GA 30122

Memo:

Signature: Paddy Singleton

1: 0686748303: 673-2856-95847

#670

Haines Professional Orthodontic Practice
3645 Market Place Blvd Suite 1A and B
Lithia Springs, GA 30344

Date 12/17/2010

Pay to the order of Precision Graphics $ 574.50

Regions Bank
608 Thornton Road, Lithia Springs, GA 30122

Memo:

Signature: Paddy Singleton

1: 0686748303: 670-2856-95847

Regions Bank- December 31, 2010 Statement page 8 of 12

#681

Haines Professional Orthodontic Practice
3645 Market Place Blvd Suite 1A and B
Lithia Springs, GA 30344

Date 12/22/2010

Pay to the order of Langley Tax + Accounting $ 160 —

Regions Bank
608 Thornton Road, Lithia Springs, GA 30122

Memo:

Signature: Paddy Singleton

1: 0686748303: 681-2856-95847

#682

Haines Professional Orthodontic Practice
3645 Market Place Blvd Suite 1A and B
Lithia Springs, GA 30344

Date 12/22/2010

Pay to the order of LSHS Booster Club $ 1,500 —

Regions Bank
608 Thornton Road, Lithia Springs, GA 30122

Memo:

Signature: Paddy Singleton

1: 0686748303: 682-2856-95847

#675

Haines Professional Orthodontic Practice
3645 Market Place Blvd Suite 1A and B
Lithia Springs, GA 30344

Date 12/25/2010

Pay to the order of Lauren Smith $ 1,620.92

Regions Bank
608 Thornton Road, Lithia Springs, GA 30122

Memo:

Signature: Paddy Singleton

1: 0686748303: 675-2856-95847

Regions Bank- December 31, 2010 Statement page 9 of 12

#676

Haines Professional Orthodontic Practice
3645 Market Place Blvd Suite 1A and B
Lithia Springs, GA 30344

Date 12/25/2010

Pay to the order of Lalie Tomah $ 1,606.17

Regions Bank
608 Thornton Road, Lithia Springs, GA 30122

Memo:

Signature: Paddy Singleton

1: 0686748303: 676-2856-95847

#677

Haines Professional Orthodontic Practice
3645 Market Place Blvd Suite 1A and B
Lithia Springs, GA 30344

Date 12/25/2010

Pay to the order of Linda Williams $ 1,657.70

Regions Bank
608 Thornton Road, Lithia Springs, GA 30122

Memo:

Signature: Paddy Singleton

1: 0686748303: 677-2856-95847

#678

Haines Professional Orthodontic Practice
3645 Market Place Blvd Suite 1A and B
Lithia Springs, GA 30344

Date 12/25/2010

Pay to the order of Carol Plumb $ 768.57

Regions Bank
608 Thornton Road, Lithia Springs, GA 30122

Memo:

Signature: Paddy Singleton

1: 0686748303: 678-2856-95847

Regions Bank- December 31, 2010 Statement page 10 of 12

#679

Haines Professional Orthodontic Practice
3645 Market Place Blvd Suite 1A and B
Lithia Springs, GA 30344

Date 12/25/2010

Pay to the order of Paddy Singleton $ 2,260.50

Regions Bank
608 Thornton Road, Lithia Springs, GA 30122

Memo:

Signature: Paddy Singleton

1: 0686748303: 679-2856-95847

#680

Haines Professional Orthodontic Practice
3645 Market Place Blvd Suite 1A and B
Lithia Springs, GA 30344

Date 12/25/2010

Pay to the order of Tamra Haines $ 8,818.75

Regions Bank
608 Thornton Road, Lithia Springs, GA 30122

Memo:

Signature: Paddy Singleton

1: 0686748303:680-2856-95847

#683

Haines Professional Orthodontic Practice
3645 Market Place Blvd Suite 1A and B
Lithia Springs, GA 30344

Date 12/22/2010

Pay to the order of Art for Kidz $ 150 –

Regions Bank
608 Thornton Road, Lithia Springs, GA 30122

Memo:

Signature: Paddy Singleton

1: 0686748303: 683-2856-95847

Regions Bank- December 31, 2010 Statement page 11 of 12

#684

Haines Professional Orthodontic Practice
3645 Market Place Blvd Suite 1A and B
Lithia Springs, GA 30344

Date 12/22/2010

Pay to the order of LS Youth Recreation $ 1,500 —

Regions Bank
608 Thornton Road, Lithia Springs, GA 30122

Memo:

Signature: Paddy Singleton

1: 0686748303: 684-2856-95847

#686

Haines Professional Orthodontic Practice
3645 Market Place Blvd Suite 1A and B
Lithia Springs, GA 30344

Date 12/29/2010

Pay to the order of Tamera Haines $ 60,000 —

Regions Bank
608 Thornton Road, Lithia Springs, GA 30122

Memo:

Signature: Paddy Singleton

1: 0686748303:686-2856-95847

#687

Haines Professional Orthodontic Practice
3645 Market Place Blvd Suite 1A and B
Lithia Springs, GA 30344

Date 12/29/2010

Pay to the order of Sams Club $ 1,000 —

Regions Bank
608 Thornton Road, Lithia Springs, GA 30122

Memo:

Signature: Paddy Singleton

1: 0686748303: 687-2856-95847

Regions Bank- December 31, 2010 Statement page 12 of 12

Exhibit 3.12b: Details of Items Noted in December Bank Statement (*Exhibit 3.12a*)

I. NSF

Two customer payments totaling $1,520 that were deposited in December were shown on the bank statement as being NSF (insufficient funds). That is, when Regions Bank presented the check payments of these two customers to their banks, it was notified that the checks could not be honored due to the existence of insufficient funds in their accounts. On January 14, 2011, Carol called the patients and subsequently, you (following in Paddy's footsteps) drove to one patient's house and picked up a new check totaling $825 (*Exhibit 3.8*). Carol was not able to track down the second patient.

II. Breakdown of Direct Deposit (DD)- Care Credit

The Care Credit deposits for December (through 12/24) had been directly deposited into the bank account (net of the service fee) on the following dates:

November charges deposited on	Thursday, December 2	$ 9,323.65
December charges deposited on	Thursday, December 2	2,671.21
	Tuesday, December 14	16,246.19
	Friday, December 24	7,581.05
	Total deposits accounted for:	35,822.10
	Plus 3% fee	1,107.90
	Total receivable collected	$36,930.00

III. CD

The CD matured on 12/31 for a total of $351,312.50 (including $1,312.50 of interest), which was credited to the account as of this date. You informed Dr. Haines. After talking to her banker (in January 2011), she purchased a new 180-day CD with a slightly higher yield.

Julia Shapland and Cynthia Turner

Project Movie Theater

Carlos Vega

4 Project Movie Theater

4 Project Movie Theater

Carlos Vega has always loved movies. As a young child growing up in Mexico City, he and his older brother spent many hot summer days in the welcoming air conditioning found in the neighborhood theater. Mexico City was home for Carlos for the first eight years of his life until his father, an executive with ADM, was transferred to Buenos Aires and then to Brazil. Another corporate transfer placed Carlos in Toledo, Ohio where he spent his high school years.

Despite being the "new kid," Carlos quickly found a peer group due to his involvement in the high school theater and music program. Carlos was quite talented and was given the lead in "West Side Story" his senior year. However, Carlos decided early on that an acting career was too much of a long shot. He was thankful, though, to his high school drama teacher for her advice and guidance. She pointed out that his voice itself was a valuable asset and introduced him to the possibility of a career as a voice-over artist. She even assisted him in obtaining an agent.

People often described Carlos's voice as "soothing yet powerful" and "deep and rumbling." Further, due to his bilingual upbringing, he could easily shift from Spanish to English. Depending on the job, he would often draw on the different local dialects that he had experienced firsthand during his childhood. Moreover, with a voice that was frequently compared to actors such as Ricardo Montalbán and Antonio Banderas, Carlos soon found his services in high demand. Carlos attended Miami University in Oxford, Ohio and paid for his college degree entirely by working as a voice-over artist for radio advertisers across the world. In 1988, he graduated with a Bachelor of Arts degree in Mass Communication, and with a minor in Linguistics. After college, he started a career in radio broadcasting.

Now 25 years later, Carlos lives in Seattle, Washington. In addition to the occasional voice-over work, he is currently a host for a successful morning radio show and has become somewhat of a

---

This course project was prepared by Julia P. Shapland and Cynthia W. Turner of the University of Illinois at Urbana-Champaign for classroom use and discussion. All businesses and characters appearing in this work are fictitious. Any resemblance to existing businesses or real persons, living or dead, is purely coincidental.

local celebrity. Carlos is married with three children and gets his acting fix by performing in local theater productions. Among other things, he continues to enjoy watching movies, which has become a favorite pastime for his family as well.

In 2008, while reading the Sunday paper, Carlos came across an article that caught his interest. Specifically, the article was about the closing of the Park Cinema, a historic single-screen movie house located in the heart of downtown Seattle.

A Newspaper Recount: The History of The Park Cinema

Originally known as the Park Theater, "The Park" has a long and glamorous history in the Seattle community dating back to its establishment in the early 1900s as a vaudeville theater. Since 1911, The Park has been in continuous use for motion picture exhibition. Although never proven, local legend holds that during the 1920s, the theater was actually a "front" for a popular prohibition-era speakeasy.

The Park continued its successful theater tenure until 1987 when the multiplex building spree reached Seattle. As would be expected, the introduction of multiplex theaters[1] into the Seattle market put many of the smaller theater owners out of business. Like its competitors, The Park suffered and quickly went from a thriving business to barely surviving.

The newspaper article explained that Martin Howell, owner of The Park Theater, recognized that the "multiplex experience was not for everyone." Thus, when multiplex theaters arrived in Seattle, he wisely reinvented The Park such that it appealed to a different customer base, particularly the avant-garde crowd. Howell found these customers to be the type who avoided movies that were a draw for mainstream pop culture. They objected to attending what they saw as "mindless" blockbuster movies, especially when packed in a large, multiplex theater with a multitude of other viewers. Consequently, to appeal to this crowd, The Park closed in 1989 for eight months during which time the beloved theater, described as a "local cinema treasure," was remodeled in an art deco modern style. The renovations included, among other things, a stylish replica of the original storefront marquee and ticket booth. The theater reopened as The Park Cinema and began a new chapter in its existence as an "art house cinema," serving a niche market in which the larger theater chains did not compete.

---

[1] A state-of-the-art movie theater containing up to 16 separate screens.

The article further explained that while the multiplex venue typically shows films that are widely released on a national or international scale, The Park Cinema shows art films with limited distribution. The art film genre tends to appeal to intellectual individuals who enjoy filmmaking as an art and appreciate such things as cinematic technique, authorial expression, and character development.

The article ended with a tribute to Howell for his numerous contributions to the arts community and a discussion of the closure of the theater. The story indicated that its closure was the result of rising operating costs, a tight economy, and the fact that Howell was getting older and could no longer manage the day-to-day operations.

Carlos knew before he had finished the article that this chance was what he had been waiting for. Together, he and his wife Tracy approached Howell to discuss purchasing the business. After a brief negotiation, they agreed to rent the building from Howell and purchase the existing equipment and supplies. The purchase agreement gave them the sole right to operate The Park Cinema. The theater opened for operations under the Vegas' management on July 1, 2009.

Operations of The Park Cinema

Movie Programming:

Carlos benefits greatly from the repeat visit of his movie patrons. In fact, he depends upon it. His market segment is small and unique. Thus, in order to generate revenue, he must entice many of the same individuals to return again and again. His small, but loyal customer base visits often, but only to the extent that he can offer them a new feature (since their last visit) and an appealing movie-going experience. In order to provide a variety of offerings with only one viewing screen, Carlos runs his films for a short time period (typically one to two weeks), which allows him to frequently show new films. He also tries to be creative in his movie selections by scouring publications, visiting film festivals, and relying on suggestions from his eclectic clientele.

Additionally, Carlos utilizes the services of Premiere Entertainment, a film-buying service, and works directly with Janet Heiser, an experienced film buyer who specializes in the art film genre. Janet not only researches possible films, but also serves as an intermediary between a number of film production companies and the theater. In many cases, Premiere decides how many prints of the film the production company should produce and determines how best to distribute them throughout the industry in order to maximize profit. Janet negotiates the terms of the contract between the production company and the movie theater and also determines how the box office proceeds will be shared or divided between the various stakeholders. The final split paid for 35-mm films is still very much dependent on these negotiations, making Janet's vast experience and strong industry relationships extremely valuable and well worth the pay.

This distribution model has been in place for many years. Nonetheless, with the introduction of digital technology, movies will be much more accessible, and the middleman/distributor's role will likely be downplayed or possibly eliminated. The digital phenomenon is transforming the industry and will allow smaller operators direct access to more content at a lower cost. However, for now, digital technology is still new to the industry, and Carlos has only recently made the decision to purchase a digital projection system.

Approximately 20 percent of The Park's ticket sales come from the "midnight movie" market. These movies are intended for a much different audience than the feature presentation. Midnight movies are run on Thursday, Friday, and Saturday evenings and typically involve an older mainstream hit, classic horror film, or the well loved "it's so bad, its good" flick such as *Zombieland.*

Revenue Sources:

The Park Cinema generates its revenue through four different sources: box office receipts (i.e., ticket sales), on-screen advertising, concession sales, and private screening / theater rental.

- *Box Office Receipts:* In order to be available to its diverse customer base, The Park does not close for major holidays and is open 7 days a week, 365 days a year.

Feature Presentation:	Everyday at 7:30 p.m. Saturday & Sunday matinees shown at 2:00 p.m.
Midnight Movie:	Special features shown Thursday, Friday, & Saturday evenings at midnight.
Special Events:	Scheduled based on theater availability.
Ticket Prices:	Senior \$6.00 / Adult \$9.00 / Child \$6.00 Student \$7.50 / Matinee \$6.50 / Midnight Movie \$5.00

Approximately 50 percent of customers pay with cash or debit cards, and 48 percent pay with credit cards. The remaining 2 percent use a loyalty card. The funds due for debit and credit card purchases are deposited directly into The Park's bank account (net of a 3 percent service fee) every 10 days or so. In addition to the 3 percent service fee, the theater must rent equipment in order to be able to swipe the card and electronically transmit the sales data. In order to help recoup these costs, Carlos has considered giving a discount for payments being made in cash.

- *On Screen Advertising (OSA):* Local businesses pay The Park $500 per month to advertise on the big screen during the time leading up to the feature presentation. In exchange, advertisers are included in a slide show of advertisements that is shown at the beginning of all movie features for the month. The amount of time given to any particular ad depends on the number of advertisers. Carlos caps the number of advertisers at five so that adequate time can be given to each. Occasionally, a local business fully sponsors a particular feature and receives full rights to all on-screen advertising for the film. Most purchases of on-screen advertising are billed on account; however, some customers occasionally pay in advance and lock in an advertising slot for months at a time. Businesses that are billed on account are expected to pay their account receivable balance in full within 30 days of being invoiced. Uncollectible accounts do happen but are rare and not very predictable.[2]

- *Concession Sales:* Due to the high profit margin, concession sales are an important element of the theater's value chain. Additionally, Carlos recognizes that his clientele are discriminating consumers and are not only interested in the quality of film, but in the quality of the entire movie-going experience. As a result, Carlos has "classed up" the concession offerings by including locally prepared gourmet baked goods and vegan offerings. The Park's client base is typically older and the inclusion of local gourmet coffee drinks and alcoholic beverages have greatly boosted sales. Carlos offers a wide array of local and imported beer and tries to purchase wine grown at local vineyards. Liquor prices are expensive given that Washington is a control state and alcoholic beverages can be purchased only at state-run liquor stores.

Concession sales received another boost when Carlos began offering his patrons the opportunity to remain after the 7:30 show and participate in a guided discussion group. During the summer of 2009, he rented space from the city of Seattle and created an

[2] Assume that the theater uses the "direct write off" method when accounting for bad debt. Under this method, bad debt expense is recorded at the time the customer receivable is written off.

outdoor patio that patrons enjoy using. The art film typically lends itself to discussion, and the sophisticated clientele enjoy the opportunity to converse about the film while having a glass wine or cup of coffee.

Concession sales (unlike box office receipts) are subject to sales tax. Carlos collects the 9.5 percent sales tax from the customer at the time of sale and is responsible for remitting the funds to the state taxing authority on a timely basis.

- *Private Screening/Theater Rental:* The Theater can seat 250 patrons. As such, local businesses frequently rent out the theater to hold corporate meetings or other special events. If the meeting includes a video presentation, the theater equipment is available for use. Local organizations also sponsor daytime showings of particular films. For example, a local church rented the theater in order to offer three separate showings of "The Blind Side" to its 700+ membership base. Some individuals rent the theater for private functions (i.e., Oscar party, World Cup) or for a private viewing of a particular film. The rental cost of the theater is $200 per hour plus reimbursement for any costs of obtaining the film or other extra services provided. The concession remains open and depending on the event, tickets may or may not be sold. Clients are expected to make a 50 percent deposit in advance of the event and then are billed for the remaining rental fee and any other charges. Similar to advertising, businesses are expected to pay their account receivable balances in full within 30 days of being invoiced.

Additionally, student groups frequently have outings at The Park. Rather than renting the facility, the students make a movie recommendation to The Park and guarantee that at least 50 people will show up. The students then pay the individual student rate rather than $200 per hour and equipment rental.

Operating Costs:

Facility Cost: The Vegas signed a three-year lease with Howell that requires quarterly rental payments of $36,000. The facility is not large, but due to its age, utilities and maintenance can be substantial. Per the terms of the lease, the 2010 required rental payments are provided in *Figure 4.1*.

Figure 4.1

Payment Due Date	Payment Amount	Coverage Period
By March 15, 2010	$36,000	April, May, and June 2010
By June 15, 2010	$36,000	July, August, and September 2010
By September 15, 2010	$36,000	October, November, and December 2010
By December 15, 2010	$36,000	January, February, and March 2011

Film Buying: As previously discussed, Carlos's film buyer (Janet Heiser with Premiere Entertainment) negotiates the terms of the contract that specify how the ticket price collected by the theater will be split between the theater, the distributor (Premiere), and the company that actually produced the movie. Carlos reports box office sales to Premiere on a weekly basis, and within 10 days of the show closing, he must remit the final payment for Premier's portion or "split" of the ticket sales. Premiere then pays the film producer out of its portion.

Under the current 35-mm film model, the typical new release film results in a 50/50 split between the theater (Carlos) and the distributor (Janet, film buyer). In the case of the more eclectic Park Cinema, the films being shown are usually older. Consequently, the split is more favorable, resulting in the theater keeping a larger share (approximately 60 percent) of the box office receipts.

In addition to the split of ticket proceeds, the theater pays Premier Entertainment $500 per month to retain its services. Additionally, as mentioned earlier, Carlos does his own research by reading various industry publications, scouring online articles, and traveling to film festivals held across the nation.

Insurance: Under the terms of the lease, the Vegas are responsible for maintaining adequate insurance coverage. They currently have three policies:

- *Building and Liability Insurance:* Covers the property's structure, furniture, equipment, and inventory. This particular policy includes added liability protection that covers personal injury or death that could occur on the premises. The building and liability insurance policy is a 9-month policy with the first $3,375 premium being paid in 2009 effective 7/1/2009. The theater did not experience a premium rate increase until the December of 2010 premium payment, renewing the policy through September 30, 2011.

- *Workers Compensation:* Required by law and covers medical expenses and at least some portion of lost wages if employees are injured on the job. Rates are based on the industry and the inherent hazards that are present. Coverage is obtained directly from the Washington State Department and quarterly premiums are paid in arrears[3] at a rate of .45 per hour worked. Between January 1 and November 30 of 2010, The Park employees worked 11,130 hours, which included 96 hours worked in November but paid in December (*Exhibit 4.7a*). Carlos accrues the workers compensation (WC) insurance expense on a monthly basis, which is typically at the time that the bi-weekly payroll reports are received and the hours worked by employees during the month are therefore known. After making this entry, the insurance expense account and the "other accrued liability" account balances are increased to include the new WC premium incurred during the month (as a result of the additional hours worked).
- *Liquor Liability (aka "Dram Shop"):* Dram shop laws allow victims of an intoxicated individual to sue the shop that served alcohol to that individual if the damage inflicted was the result of intoxication. Dram shop insurance is an insurance policy carried by alcohol-serving establishments to cover them in the event of dram shop law violations or liability for the actions of an intoxicated patron or employee. The liquor liability insurance policy is a 12-month policy with the first $3,420 premium being paid in 2009 effective 7/1/2009. The premium rate remained unchanged for the 2010 renewal effective 7/1/2010.

Payroll: The Park has 8 part-time employees, plus the theater manager Matt who works 40+ hours per week. The "concession-only" employees are paid slightly above minimum wage while the employees that have been trained to work the projector system are paid more. The employees are paid on the second and fourth Saturday of the month. Depending on his other commitments, Carlos works about 15-20 hours per week at the theater. He does not pay himself a salary, but starting in 2009, he began taking a $2,500 per month dividend.

[3] For example, the insurance premium for the fourth quarter of 2010 is due in January 2011 when the final number of hours worked during the last 3 months of 2010 is known with certainty.

Marketing:

- *Reaching existing customers:* An important element of the theater's business plan is to encourage frequent visits from the regular theater patrons. In addition to reaching these individuals through email notifications and social networking, The Park uses what they call "loyalty cards." Similar to gift cards, these reloadable smart cards are purchased at the Park in $50 increments and can be used to pay for tickets and concession items. The cards do not expire.

  Each time a $50 card is purchased; $55 of value is loaded on the card providing the patron with an extra $5 to spend on tickets and concession. Like all loyalty card purchases, the Park is obligated to honor the total value placed on the card.

  The extra $5 placed on the card, referred to by Carlos as the "loyalty card premium," is costly for the theater to provide but well worth it considering that it directly benefits the "frequent movie goer," the most important segment of the Park's small customer base.

- *Reaching new customers:* In order to reach its target audience and expand its customer base, The Park does a substantial amount of advertising both in print and in media. The Park offers cross promotions with popular local take-out restaurants. It also advertises on the radio, in various local news publications, and on websites frequented by the arts crowd.

Theater Equipment: The Vegas purchased the theater equipment from Howell and depreciate it straight-line.

Concession: The Theater purchases concession supplies in bulk on a monthly basis from Northwest Concession Supply Company (NWCS). All purchases from NWCS are made on account. Fresh baked specialty items, including their famous cupcakes, are delivered daily from the Three Girls Bakery. Beer and liquor are purchased directly by Matt or Carlos from the local stores controlled by the Washington State Liquor Control Board. The Park makes payments using the following three methods:

- Corporate check.
- Corporate credit card for purchases of office and concession supplies as well as beer and wine.

- Register drawer for the occasional time that cash is needed.

Operating Procedures

For each show, Carlos schedules four employees, at least one of which is trained to use the projector system:

- One employee is stationed at the ticket booth to ring up sales.
- One employee is stationed directly inside the entrance of the theater to collect ticket stubs and answer patron questions.
- Two employees work the concession stand.

Matt or one of three other trained employees is in charge of the projection booth equipment. Employees must arrive at the theater at least 45 minutes before showtime and stay after to clean. On a daily basis, the theater manager prepares the film, fills the concession refrigerators, accepts delivery of concession supplies, clears the register system, and stocks all three register drawers with $700 dollars cash from the safe.

Box Office Sales:

The sales cycle begins by the customer sale being rung up on the ticket booth register system by employee #1. The Park does not accept checks except from businesses that are being billed on account (theater rental and OSA). The ticket booth register system automatically prints the ticket as a result of the sale being rung up. The entire register system is web-based, and the daily sales data can be conveniently accessed from any location. Once he or she has received a ticket, the customer enters the theater and is met by employee #2 who looks at the ticket, verifies the show and date, and then tears off the top portion of the ticket and returns the bottom portion or "ticket stub" to the customer as proof of payment. The customer then enters the concession line or goes directly to the theater.

Once the movie has started, the top portions of all the tickets are given to the manager who will count them and compare the total number to the daily sale data per the register system.

Concession Sales:

The concession area has two register systems with an employee assigned to each. Like the ticket booth, checks are not accepted. The register system tracks sales but does not provide details of which individual items have been sold. Instead, Carlos and Matt must count the concession items before the start of business on the first day of each month. Given the new concession purchases made during the month, they can then determine the total cost of the concession items sold as shown in *Figure 4.2*.[4]

Figure 4.2

	Candy & Snack	Alcoholic Beverages	Non-Alcoholic Beverages	Concession Supplies	Total
Cost of concession items on hand, 1/1	$ 1,879.58	$ 1,611.96	$ 1,422.08	$1,104.31	$ 6,017.93
Plus: New purchases made (1/1-11/30)	23,850.54	37,967.25	26,429.43	4,164.61	92,411.83
Equals: Total items available to be sold	25,730.12	39,579.21	27,851.51	5,268.92	98,429.76
Less: Items counted on 11/30/10	(2,020.50)	(1,406.73)	(1,605.25)	(980.82)	(6,013.30)
Cost of concession items sold (1/1–11/30)	$23,709.62	$38,172.48	$26,246.26	$4,288.10	$ 92,416.46

At the end of each evening, the cash in each of the three register drawers is counted and a daily cash count sheet is updated by the employee. Matt verifies the count, and both he and the employee working the registers initial the report, which is scanned and emailed to Tracy, Carlos's wife. Matt separates out the original $2,100 register cash ($700 each) to use the next day and locks all the funds in the safe. Carlos comes into the office frequently to pay bills and make the bank deposit.

Tracy accesses the register data from home on a daily basis and uses the information to prepare the following two reports:

- *Box Office Summary Sheet:* This report summarizes the number and type of tickets sold on a particular day representing the total daily sales per the register system. Tracy prepares one of these reports for each feature film and includes the data for the midnight movies shown during the same time frame. In addition to being used internally, the data per this report is provided to Premier Entertainment as the basis for calculating the amount owed for the negotiated box office split.
- *Payment Summary:* Based on the register data, this report details the total sales by payment type (i.e. cash, debit card, credit card, or loyalty card). For each date, Tracy compares the total cash counted in the register drawers to the register sales in order to determine by how much (if any) the register drawer was over (or short) in a particular

[4] This is known as a periodic inventory system.

day. Mistakes happen and minor differences are expected to occur but larger differences are taken out of the employee's pay. This type of adjustment is rarely necessary, and these nominal cash overages/shortages are regularly written off to Miscellaneous Expense. Tracy frequently accesses the corporate bank account online and makes sure that (i) the deposits being made are equal to the cash being reported as collected and (ii) the amounts owed for debit and credit card sales are in fact being received on a timely basis.

Accounting System

Initially, Tracy came in weekly and updated the accounting software for the business transactions. However, as the business grew, more than a weekly visit was needed, and Tracy trained Matt (the theater manager) to maintain the books. Matt began managing the books on February 1, 2010.

In the past, Carlos had not prepared any formal financial statement. Instead, standalone reports and spreadsheets were generated from the accounting software and provided to the outside accountants to use while preparing the annual tax returns.

This year, things have changed. In mid-2010, Mr. Howell approached Carlos about investing in the theater. Carlos recognizes that while he would be giving up some control, he would also be bringing on an extremely knowledgeable business partner. Over the next 18 months, Carlos anticipates that the 20+ year old Art Deco building façade will require some substantial improvements, not to mention the more imminent cost of upgrading to digital technology. From Carlos's perspective, it would be nice to have some additional capital to fund these improvements. As part of the process, Mr. Howell has asked that he be provided with a complete set of accrual financial statements. Specifically, he would like to receive an Income Statement, a Statement of Equity, and a Statement of Cash Flow for the 12 months ended December 31, 2010 and a classified Balance Sheet dated as of December 31, 2010.

Case 4-1

Classifying Financial Statement Elements

(and working with the balance sheet equation)

You have been provided with the following items:

- *Exhibit 4.1*: A listing of the individual account balances reported on The Park Cinema's 11/30/10 trial balance. The balances shown in *Exhibit 4.1* are for the 11 months ended 11/30/10. Except as noted for Retained Earnings, all accounts have normal balances (that is, account balances that are expected to carry a debit balance have a debit balance and vice versa). Further, please note that this exhibit provides you with *a description* of the underlying account rather than an actual account title (such as Accounts Receivable, Accounts Payable, Rent Expense, and so forth). Each description represents one single account from either the Balance Sheet (such as an asset, liability, or equity account), or from the Income Statement (in which it measures either revenues earned or expenses incurred from January through November 2010).
- *Exhibit 4.2*: Equipment listing and depreciation schedule.
- *Exhibit 4.3*: Physical count of concession items on hand as of 11/30.
- *Exhibit 4.4*: Movie listing and split summary for movies shown from January 1 to November 30, 2010.

Requirements:

1. Use the ***Narrative*** to classify each account listed in *Exhibit 4.1* as an asset, liability, equity, revenue, or expense account. When submitting this requirement, please list the accounts in numeric order, using the account reference numbers provided in the first column of *Exhibit 4.1*.

2. Prepare an 11/30/10 trial balance using the figures provided in *Exhibit 4.1* and your account classification from requirement (1). The cash balance has been intentionally omitted from this listing. Please solve for the missing cash balance and include this amount in your trial balance. When submitting this requirement, please sort the accounts in numeric order using the account reference numbers provided in *Exhibit 4.1*.

3. Using your final trial balance from requirement (2), compute the following items (and show all work):

    a. Total equity as of 11/30/2010 (using the balance sheet equation).

    b. Net income for the 11 months ending 11/30/10.

4. Using the balance you computed for total equity in requirement (3a), determine how much of this balance is:

    a. Total contributed capital.

    b. Total retained earnings.

5. Please consider the account titled "Retained Earnings, *deficit* as of 1/1/2010." What does this account balance communicate about 2009's financial performance? Why is this number different than your calculation for the prior requirement (4b)? Explain.

6. Please consider the following stakeholders mentioned in the narrative and identify them as either an internal or external decision maker. Secondly, for each decision maker listed, provide a specific example of how they in particular could be harmed (as a result of faulty decision making) if the financial information being reported to them by The Park Cinema was later found to be inaccurate.

    a. Carlos Vega

    b. Premier Entertainment

    c. Mr. Howell

    d. Washington state taxing authority

    e. NCH Bank

Case 4-2

Analyzing Monthly Transactions

Soon after starting your second semester junior year in Accountancy at the Albers School of Business at the University of Seattle, you learn that The Park Cinema is looking to hire an accounting intern. During your interview with Carlos, he explains that he needs to provide a potential investor with 2010 financial statements as soon as possible. He also explains that Matt (the theater manager) who normally handles the books has been working reduced hours due to the birth of his first child, and as a result, he has not yet recorded any of the December transaction activity. Given that time is of the essence, Carlos has decided to hire an accounting intern to complete these tasks. You see this opportunity as a great way to practice your accounting fundamentals while enhancing your resume. You accept Carlos's offer and get to work right away.

In order to assist you in your work, Carlos has provided you with the following items:

- *Exhibit 4.5*: Although Matt did not record any December transactions, both he and Carlos kept detailed notes regarding the transactions and events that took place in December. This exhibit represents a combined summary of their notes.
- *Exhibit 4.6a and 4.6b*: Northwest Concession Supply Invoices (12/6 & 12/17).
- *Exhibit 4.7a and 4.7b*: December Payroll Reports.
- *Exhibit 4.8a and 4.8b*: Box Office Summary Sheets (*Solitary Man*) and (*127 Hours*).
- *Exhibit TN 4.1*: The 11/30/2010 trial balance ***(available from your instructor)***. *(These balances should be used as your beginning account balances.)*

Requirements:

1. Referring back to the ***Narrative*** as needed, please prepare journal entries (using good form) *as necessary* for the December transactions and events described in the accompanying exhibits for this case. That is, you should prepare only those *specific* entries required to

record the transactions described in these materials. You are not to consider adjusting entries that would be recorded after the events described in these exhibits.[1]

2. Using the journal entries that you prepared in requirement (1), post the entries to "T" accounts and calculate the overall account balances.

3. Using the ending balances in the "T" accounts from requirement (2), prepare a 12/31/10 unadjusted trial balance for The Park Cinema. Please provide a summary detailing all items you have recorded in "other accrued liabilities" and in "miscellaneous expense."

4. Consider whether any account balance in the unadjusted trial balance prepared in requirement (3) is abnormal. (That is, an account balance that is expected to carry a debit balance has a credit balance and vice versa.) If you determine that a particular account balance is abnormal, label it as such and explain what the abnormal balance communicates.

5. Briefly describe the prepaid advertising account, how it is used, and how it is different than the advertising expense account. Will a company that incurs advertising costs always have a prepaid advertising account? Explain.

6. Revisit the unadjusted trial balance you prepared in requirement (3). Select two balance sheet accounts that you believe will ultimately require an adjusting entry. (Remember, you are not recording adjusting entries in this case.) When making your two selections, be sure to identify at least one account in which the adjusting entry will help The Park Cinema more fully achieve the "realization" and/or the "matching" principles, and explain why this is so.

   - For each account balance, propose the entries you anticipate you will make and explain why they are necessary. (Again, remember to explain how the "realization" and/or the "matching" principles are more fully achieved for at least one of these entries.) In your discussion, please comment if there is additional information that you would need in order to make your entry.

[1] Please use the account titles listed in *Exhibit TN 4.1* for purposes of your entries. If you need to create a new account, please do so, but, clearly label it as to its type (asset, liability, equity, revenue, or expense). You may also find it helpful to review the detailed descriptions of the 11/30 account balances contained in *Exhibit 4.1*.

Case 4-3

Recording Year-End Adjustments

You are in your second semester junior year in the accountancy department at the Albers School of Business at the University of Seattle, and are currently working as an accounting intern for Carlos Vega, owner of The Park Cinema. You have been hired because the theater manager Matt (who normally handles the books) has been, and will continue to be, on personal leave for some time, and Carlos needs to provide 2010 financial statements to a potential investor as soon as possible. To date, you have assisted Carlos by recording The Park Cinema's December transactions, and you are now ready to prepare the December adjusting entries.

Carlos provides the following items to assist you in preparing the year-end adjustments.

- *Exhibit 4.9*: Summary of events that took place during the first two weeks of January 2011.
- *Exhibit 4.10*: Northwest Concession Supply Invoice (12/31).
- *Exhibit 4.11*: January 2011 Payroll Report.
- *Exhibit 4.12*: Kardwell Custom Design Invoice.
- *Exhibit 4.13*: Start-up Loan Amortization Schedule.
- *Exhibit 4.14*: Box Office Summary Sheet (*The Girl Who Kicked the Hornets' Nest*).
- *Exhibit 4.15*: December Corporate Credit Card Statement.
- *Exhibit TN 4.2*: The 12/31/10 unadjusted trial balance for the theater (***available from your instructor***). *(These balances should be used as your beginning account balances.)*
- *Exhibit TN 4.3:* This exhibit will be made available by the instructor to students who are ***not*** completing ***Case 4-4***. See footnote 3 (on the next page) for more details.

Requirements:

Carlos asks that you make *all* adjustments that are necessary in order to produce proper accrual basis financial statements.[1] Specifically, you are to complete the following.

1. Determine which 12/31/10 account balances (*Exhibit TN 4.2*) require adjustment and prepare the required adjusting journal entries.[2]

2. Post the adjusting journal entries from requirement (1) to "T" accounts and calculate the overall account balances.

3. Use the ending balances in the "T" accounts from requirement (2) to prepare a 12/31/10 adjusted trial balance for The Park Cinema.[3] Please provide a breakdown of the items being included in "other accrued liabilities" and in "miscellaneous expense."

4. Consider the Vegas' personal charges on the corporate credit card as well as the travel cost for Tracy to accompany Carlos to Minneapolis. Using the accounts listed in *Exhibit TN 4.2*, provide at least two possible alternatives for the debit portion of the resulting journal entry(ies) and explain how the economic entity assumption impacts your choices. Given your two options, please clarify what additional information you would need from Carlos in order to determine which specific classification best captures the economic reality of this situation.

5. As of 1/1/10, the theater reported $2,835 of prepaid insurance as a current asset on its balance sheet. Remember that the prepaid insurance account balance is made up of two separate policies: a 9-month building and liability policy and a 12-month liquor liability (dram shop) policy. ***Case 4-2*** included an entry to record the insurance payment made on 12/21/10 (*Exhibit 4.5*) to renew the building liability policy. Given this information as well as that provided in the ***Narrative***, prepare the following:

---

[1] After considering the information provided in the accompanying exhibits, determine whether there are any *additional* adjustments that need to be made in order to produce proper accrual basis financial statements. Start by going through the unadjusted trial balance in *Exhibit TN 4.2* and for each account balance ask yourself, "Is this a deferred revenue or expense?" If so, then determine whether the account balance requires adjustment as of 12/31/10. For each of the remaining accounts, then ask yourself, "Is there any accrued revenue or accrued expense related to this account that still needs to be recorded?"

[2] Please use the account titles listed in *Exhibit TN 4.2* for purposes of your entries. If you need to create a new account, please do so, but clearly label it as to its type (asset, liability, equity, revenue, or expense). You may also find it helpful to review the detailed descriptions of the 11/30 account balances contained in *Exhibit 4.1*.

[3] If you are required to complete ***Case 4-4***, you will prepare additional adjusting entries as a result of the information provided in that case, and your adjusted trial balance will accordingly not be finalized until after these additional entries. If you are not required to complete ***Case 4-4***, you should receive *Exhibit TN 4.3* from your instructor which will provide you with the necessary information to prepare all adjusting entries as well as your final adjusted trial balance.

a. Complete the following analysis for the insurance expense account:

	Insurance Expense Recorded		
	1/1 to 11/30	12/1-12/31	Total
Building Liability	?	?	?
Liquor Liability (DRAM)	?	?	?
Workers Compensation	?	?[4]	?
Total Insurance Expense	?[5]	?	?

b. Complete the following analysis for the prepaid insurance account:

	Building	**DRAM**	**Total**
Prepaid insurance as of 1/1/10	?	?	$2,835.00[6]
Insurance coverage renewals (1/1/10 to 11/30/10)	?	?	?
Insurance coverage expired (1/1/10 to 11/30/10)	(?)	(?)	(?)[7]
Prepaid insurance balance as of 11/30/2010	?	?	?[7]
Insurance coverage renewals (12/1/10 to 12/31/10)	?	?	?
Insurance coverage expired (12/1/10 to 12/31/10)	(?)	(?)	(?)
Prepaid insurance balance as of 12/31/10	?	?	?

You should assume that all insurance policies have been renewed at the end of the policy term. Further, in order to earn any credit, you must show all work.

6. Please consider the accounting treatment surrounding the three insurance policies. For each of the three insurance policies:

   a. Identify whether the accounting treatment would result in the recording of a deferred expense or an accrued expense.

   b. Discuss how the accounting treatment selected in the previous requirement (a) (deferred expense or accrued expense) will impact the underlying financial statements.

[4] As noted in the ***Narrative***, worker's compensation is accrued at the time the employees are paid and, therefore, the hours worked are known. Details about the hours worked in December can be seen in *Exhibits 4.7a, 4.7b, and 4.11*.

[5] You are encouraged to utilize the relevant balances reported in *Exhibit 4.1* as check figures.

[6] Given the information provided in the ***Narrative*** and *Exhibit 4.5* (12/6 (ii) meeting and 12/21 (iv) insurance renewal), calculate the portion of each policy that should have still been prepaid at 1/1/2010. Roll the account balance forward to 11/30, and then again to 12/31 using the template provided here.

[7] You are encouraged to utilize the relevant balances reported in *Exhibit 4.1* as check figures.

c. Discuss why, given the nature of the underlying insurance contract,[8] this accounting treatment (deferred expense or accrued expense) is appropriate for the particular policy.

d. Contrast how the accounting treatment would be different if the policy were instead accounted for using the cash basis.

(i) How would the financial statements change?

(ii) Which method (accrual versus cash basis) helps the theater better achieve matching? Explain.

[8] Consider the timing of the cash payments required by the policy as compared to the timing of the underlying insurance coverage being received in return. Policy terms can be obtained from the ***Narrative*** and *Exhibit 4.5* (12/6 (ii) meeting and 12/21 (iv) insurance renewal).

Case 4-4

Preparing the Bank Reconciliation

As an accounting intern for The Park Cinema, you have enjoyed your experience working with local celebrity and theater owner Carlos Vega. You have been working at The Park Cinema since early January 2011, and have assisted Carlos in providing potential investor Mr. Howell with 2010 financial statements. Today, you will prepare the December bank reconciliation so that you can finalize the December adjustments. Carlos has provided you with the following items to assist you in this task.

- *Exhibit 4.16*: The November bank reconciliation (prepared by Matt, the theater manager).
- *Exhibit 4.17a*: The December bank statement received in the mail in early January 2011 (prepared by the bank).
- *Exhibit 4.17b*: Details of items noted in the December bank statement.
- *Exhibit TN 4.4*: The checkbook maintained by Carlos ***(available from your instructor)***.[1]
- *Exhibit TN 4.5*: Details of the general ledger cash balance reported in *Exhibit TN 4.6* (needed for requirement (2) only— ***available from your instructor***).
- *Exhibit TN 4.6*: The 12/31/2010 account balances that include all necessary adjusting entries *except* those additional entries that will be recorded in this case ***(available from your instructor)***.

Requirements:

1. Prepare the December bank reconciliation, reconciling the checkbook provided in *Exhibit TN 4.4* to the bank statement provided in *Exhibit 4.17a*. A reconciliation template has been provided for your use on the subsequent pages. Be sure to clearly explain all reconciling items, and when determining the nature of certain reconciling items, please note that the bank *has not* made any errors in reporting the December activity.

[1] Note that bank deposits made after 4:00 p.m. are not credited to the account by the bank until the following business day.

2. Please complete the following:

    a. Compare the final reconciled checkbook balance (that is, the final answer from requirement (1)) to the cash balance reported on the general ledger (*Exhibits TN 4.5* and *4.6*), and explain all differences noted (if any).

    b. Prepare all adjusting entries that are necessary as a result of the bank reconciliation process.[2]

3. Consider the December bank statement (*Exhibit 4.17a*). When the checks cleared the bank and the related monies were deducted from the checking account, these transactions were recorded as "debit" entries on the bank statement. You are likely familiar with a "debit card," which allows you to immediately withdraw cash from your personal bank account. We have learned in class that a positive cash balance is an asset, and that an asset's balance decreases with a credit entry and increases with a debit entry. If this is the case, why do banks refer to such withdrawals (account reductions) as "debits?" Please explain.

[2] Please provide a thorough description of all proposed entries and use the account titles listed in *Exhibit TN 4.6* for purposes of your entries. If you need to create a new account, please do so, but clearly label it as to its type (asset, liability, equity, revenue, or expense).

Bank Balance per 12/31 Bank Statement $ 28,844.28

Plus: Deposits in Transit (list individually)

Errors and other items (list individually and explain):

Explanation

Less: Outstanding Checks (list individually)

Errors and other items (list individually and explain):

Explanation

Reconciled Balance per Bank at 12/31 $

Unadjusted Balance per Checkbook at 12/31 $ (34,204.40)

Plus: Interest earned during December ________________

Errors and other items (list individually and explain):

Explanation

________________ ________________

________________ ________________

________________ ________________

________________ ________________

Less: Bank Service Fee ________________

Errors and other items (list individually and explain):

Explanation

________________ ________________

________________ ________________

________________ ________________

________________ ________________

Reconciled Balance per Checkbook at 12/31 $________________

Case 4-5

Preparing the Financial Statements

You are nearing the end of your accounting internship at The Park Cinema, and you are grateful to owner Carlos Vega for the significant role he has allowed you to play in the accounting operations as a result of his theater manager Matt having to go on personal leave. You have gained invaluable experience during your internship. Specifically, while working at The Park Cinema, you have analyzed December 2010 transactions and events, and prepared and posted journal entries (including year-end adjustments). You must now complete your final task and prepare The Park Cinema's December 31, 2010 financial statements. Carlos is anxious to provide these financials to potential investor Mr. Howell, and has provided you with the following item in order to assist you with this task.

- *Exhibit TN 4.7*: The final 12/31/2010 account balances after all adjusting entries ***(available from your instructor)***.

Requirements:

1. Using good form, prepare the following December 31, 2010 financial statements:[1]
   a. The Balance Sheet.
   b. The Income Statement (for the 12 months ended).
   c. The Statement of Shareholder's Equity (for the 12 months ended).[2]
2. Prepare all necessary closing entries.
3. Prepare a post-closing trial balance *(in good form)*.

[1] In order to determine the proper classification of the account balances included in *Exhibit TN 4.7*, you are encouraged to review the ***Narrative*** and, if necessary, information provided in *Exhibits 4.1-4.17b*.

[2] Please note that Carlos has not made any additional capital contributions during the year.

Case 4-6

Analyzing Cash Flows

It seemed like it was only yesterday that you were hired by owner Carlos Vega as an accounting intern at The Park Cinema. Having now gone through the full accounting processing cycle, you realize that you need only prepare one remaining accrual basis statement, a Statement of Cash Flow. Upon completion of this financial statement, your accounting internship at The Park Cinema will come to an end. To prepare for your final assignment, you have begun your analysis of the cash flow activity for the year ended 12/31/2010 and have gathered the following items (***to be provided by your instructor***):

- *Exhibit TN 4.8a*: A Comparative 12/31 Balance Sheet for 2009 and 2010.
- *Exhibit TN 4.8b*: The Income Statement for the 12 months ended 12/31/2010.
- *Exhibit TN 4.8c*: The Statement of Equity for the 12 months ended 12/31/2010.
- *Exhibit TN 4.9*: Other Additional Information.
- *Exhibit TN 4.10*: Sources and Uses of Cash Schedule.

Requirement:

Using "T" account analysis, complete the Sources and Uses of Cash Schedule presented in *Exhibit TN 4.10* ***(available from your instructor)***. In order to earn *any* credit you must clearly document all work, label account titles, reference the source of the information included in your "T" accounts, and show all calculations.

Exhibit 4.1: Account Listing

Ref. No.	Account Description	11/30/2010 balance
1	2010 Depreciation (*Exhibit 4.2*).	$20,812.28
2	Alcoholic beverages owned as of 11/30/2010 for concession sale (*Exhibit 4.3*).	1,406.73
3	Amount owed to Premier Entertainment for its split of ticket sales (*Exhibit 4.4*).	3,556.00
4	Amount owed to vendor Northwest Supplies.	2,775.00
5	Amount owed to Visa for charges made on the corporate credit card.	3,899.00
6	Amounts due from banks for theater patron purchases using debit cards.	8,759.91
7	Amounts due from credit card companies for theater patron purchases.	15,143.94
8	Amounts due from local businesses for purchases of on screen advertising.	2,500.00
9	Amounts owed for various small items (*see description of items at* *).	2,285.64
10	Amounts owed to employees for hours worked in November, but not yet paid.	948.50
11	Candy and snack items owned as of 11/30/2010 for concession sale (*Exhibit 4.3*).	2,020.50
12	**Cash balance (solve for unknown).**	**?**
13	Concession and ticketing equipment owned as of 11/30/2010 (*Exhibit 4.2*).	22,550.00
14	Concession supplies owned as of 11/30/2010 (*Exhibit 4.3*).	980.82
15	Cost of 10% loyalty premium added to loyalty cards during 2010.	1,540.00
16	Cost of weekly cleaning service.	3,575.00
17	Cost of 3% service fee assessed on debit and/or credit card purchases.	15,553.65
18	Cost of future advertising purchased by the Park Cinema.	9,000.00
19	Cost of building rental.	132,000.00
20	Cost of film buyer fee, travel to film festivals, and industry journals.	6,825.00
21	Cost of insurance coverage expiring in 2010.	12,268.50
22	Cost of insurance premiums purchased; coverage not yet expired.	2,370.00
23	Cost of liquor license and other fees incurred in 2010.	3,125.00
24	Cost of outdoor patio rental and occasional special event equipment rental.	6,357.00
25	Cost of outside accounting and legal services.	2,900.00
26	Cost of Park Cinema advertisements run during 2010.	49,250.00
27	Cost of repairs and maintenance to the building and equipment.	5,876.00
28	Cost of shipping movies back to distributors during 2010.	4,678.00
29	Cost of supplies consumed during 2010.	5,225.00
30	Cost of total 2010 ticket sales belonging to Premier Entertainment (*Exhibit 4.4*).	155,729.20
31	Cost of utilities consumed during 2010.	13,495.00
32	Cost of various small items such as the monthly bank service fee.	3,483.50
33	Cost of wages earned by employees during 2010.	103,524.50
34	Cumulative depreciation taken on equipment, to date (*Exhibit 4.2*).	30,918.42
35	Dividends paid to Carlos in 2010.	27,500.00
36	Historical cost of concession items sold during 2010 (*Figure 4.2*).	92,416.46

(cont'd)

Ref. No.	Account Description	11/30/2010 balance
37	Initial capital contribution made by Carlos in exchange for 100% of the stock.	25,000.00
38	Non-alcoholic beverages owned as of 11/30/2010 for concession sale (*Exhibit 4.3*).	1,605.25
39	Obligation to customers to honor prepaid customer loyalty card balances.	4,095.00
40	Obligation to outside businesses for advance payments (for OSA & theater rental).	-
41	Other supplies owned as of 11/30/2010 (*Exhibit 4.3*).	804.97
42	Portion of fourth quarter advance rent payment remaining for December of 2010.	12,000.00
43	Projection booth equipment owned as of 11/30/2010 (*Exhibit 4.2*).	39,250.00
44	Remaining principal balance owed to NCH Bank on a $75,000, 7% start up loan.	66,573.19
45	Retained Earnings, *deficit* as of 1/1/2010.	28,593.49
46	Theater equipment owned as of 11/30/2010 (*Exhibit 4.2*).	10,350.00
47	Value of all movie tickets sold during 2010 (*Exhibit 4.4*).	389,323.00
48	Value of concession items sold during 2010.	290,896.43
49	Value of OSA shown during 2010.	16,500.00
50	Value of theater rentals and special events held during 2010.	14,400.00

*Description of amounts owed for various small items (Item #9):	
November utilities due in December.	$ 875.00
October and November workers comp. insurance premiums due in January 2011.	910.64
Premier Entertainment November fees due in December.	500.00
	$2,285.64

Exhibit 4.2: Equipment Listing and Depreciation Schedule

	Acquisiton Date	Original Cost	Accum. Deprec. 12/31/2009	2010 Depreciation Jan.-Nov.	2010 Depreciation Dec.	Accum. Deprec. 11/30/2010	Accum. Deprec. 12/31/2010
Projection Booth Equipment							
Dolby Cinema Processor	*	$ 13,000.00	$ 1,986.10	$ 3,972.21	$ 361.11	$ 5,958.31	$ 6,319.42
6 power amps	*	$ 5,750.00	$ 878.46	$ 1,756.92	$ 159.72	$ 2,635.38	$ 2,795.10
Rack	*	$ 1,200.00	$ 183.32	$ 366.63	$ 33.33	$ 549.95	$ 583.28
Crossover	*	$ 1,300.00	$ 198.61	$ 397.21	$ 36.11	$ 595.82	$ 631.93
Lamp & Rectifier	*	$ 5,500.00	$ 840.29	$ 1,680.58	$ 152.78	$ 2,520.87	$ 2,673.65
Bulbs	*	$ 2,000.00	$ 305.58	$ 611.16	$ 55.56	$ 916.74	$ 972.30
Platter	*	$ 4,000.00	$ 611.10	$ 1,222.21	$ 111.11	$ 1,833.31	$ 1,944.42
Lensing	*	$ 6,500.00	$ 993.08	$ 1,986.16	$ 180.56	$ 2,979.24	$ 3,159.80
Total		$ 39,250.00					
Details on Speakers		**Price**					
3 JBL 3632 (priced @ $1,700 each)	*	$ 5,100.00	$ 779.18	$ 1,558.37	$ 141.67	$ 2,337.55	$ 2,479.22
10 surrounds at $200 each	*	$ 2,000.00	$ 305.58	$ 611.16	$ 55.56	$ 916.74	$ 972.30
Total		$ 7,100.00					
Details on Theater - Other Equipment		**Price**					
System for hearing impaired	*	$ 500.00	$ 76.39	$ 152.79	$ 13.89	$ 229.18	$ 243.07
5 Seats	*	$ 250.00	$ 38.17	$ 76.34	$ 6.94	$ 114.51	$ 121.45
Screen plus installation	*	$ 2,500.00	$ 381.92	$ 763.84	$ 69.44	$ 1,145.76	$ 1,215.20
Total		$ 3,250.00					
Concession & Ticketing Equipment		**Price**					
Popcorn Machine	*	$ 2,500.00	$ 381.92	$ 763.84	$ 69.44	$ 1,145.76	$ 1,215.20
Small refrigerator	*	$ 400.00	$ 61.10	$ 122.21	$ 11.11	$ 183.31	$ 194.42
Small freezer (under oven)	*	$ 500.00	$ 76.40	$ 152.79	$ 13.89	$ 229.19	$ 243.08
Big Freezer	*	$ 2,650.00	$ 404.85	$ 809.71	$ 73.61	$ 1,214.56	$ 1,288.17
Coffee Maker (with two 12-cup decanters)	*	$ 200.00	$ 30.53	$ 61.05	$ 5.55	$ 91.58	$ 97.13
Registers	*	$ 4,500.00	$ 687.50	$ 1,375.00	$ 125.00	$ 2,062.50	$ 2,187.50
Touch-Screen monitors	*	$ 2,000.00	$ 305.53	$ 611.05	$ 55.55	$ 916.58	$ 972.13
Credit card readers	*	$ 400.00	$ 61.11	$ 122.21	$ 11.11	$ 183.32	$ 194.43
Ticketing System	*	$ 3,400.00	$ 519.42	$ 1,038.84	$ 94.44	$ 1,558.26	$ 1,652.70
Patio Furniture	5/30/2010	$ 6,000.00	$ -	$ 600.00	$ 100.00	$ 600.00	$ 700.00
Total		$ 22,550.00					
Grand Total		$ 72,150.00	$ 10,106.14	$ 20,812.28	$ 1,937.48	$ 30,918.42	$ 32,855.90

* acquired from Mr. Howell on 7/1/2009

Projection Booth	$ 39,250.00
Theater Equipment	$ 10,350.00
Concession Equipment	$ 22,550.00
	$ 72,150.00

Exhibit 4.3: Physical Count of Concession Stand as of 11/30

		Unit Price	Quantity In Stock	Value as of 11/30
Candy/Snacks				
Junior Mints	Quantity Per Box	24.00		
	Case	$ 25.73	2.75	$ 70.76
	Individual Boxes	$ 1.07	12.00	$ 12.87
Milk Duds	Quantity Per Box	48.00		
	Case	$ 35.59	1.75	$ 62.28
	Individual Boxes	$ 0.7415	32.00	$ 23.73
Goobers	Quantity Per Box	60.00		
	Case	$ 48.08	3.00	$ 144.24
	Individual Boxes	$ 0.8013	24.00	$ 19.23
Twizzlers	Quantity Per Box	60.00		
	Case	$ 44.35	3.75	$ 166.31
	Individual Boxes	$ 0.7391	54.00	$ 39.91
Dots	Quantity Per Box	24.00		
	Case	$ 20.90	2.75	$ 57.48
	Individual Boxes	$ 0.8708	21.00	$ 18.29
Reeses Pieces	Quantity Per Box	24.00		
	Case	$ 28.82	3.00	$ 86.46
	Individual Boxes	$ 1.2011	18.00	$ 21.62
Raisinettes	Quantity Per Box	60.00		
	Case	$ 48.08	2.75	$ 132.22
	Individual Boxes	$ 0.8013	45.00	$ 36.06
Buncha Crunch	Quantity Per Box	48.00		
	Case	$ 38.47	2.25	$ 86.56
	Individual Boxes	$ 0.8017	32.00	$ 25.65
Sno Caps	Quantity Per Box	60.00		
	Case	$ 48.08	4.00	$ 192.32
	Individual Boxes	$ 0.8013	12.00	$ 9.62
Sour Patch Kids	Quantity Per Box	60.00		
	Case	$ 35.86	1.50	$ 53.79
	Individual Boxes	$ 0.5977	32.00	$ 19.13
Dry-Roasted Peanuts	Quantity Per Box	144.00		
	Case	$ 44.59	1.00	$ 44.59
	Individual Boxes	$ 0.3097	45.00	$ 13.94
Kellog's Fruit Snacks	Quantity Per Box	48.00		
	Case	$ 19.05	2.00	$ 38.10
	Individual Boxes	$ 0.3969	26.00	$ 10.32
Wasabi Rice Crackers	Quantity Per Box	72.00		
	Case	$ 26.73	1.00	$ 26.73
	Individual Boxes	$ 0.3713	9.00	$ 3.34
Cookie Dough Bites	Quantity Per Box	144.00		
	Case	$ 73.81	2.50	$ 184.53
	Individual Boxes	$ 0.5126	92.00	$ 47.16

Exhibit 4.3: Physical Count of Concession Stand as of 11/30 (cont'd)

		Unit Price	Quantity In Stock	Value as of 11/30
Mini Pretzels	Quantity Per Box	48.00		
	Case	$ 17.73	2.00	$ 35.46
	Individual Boxes	$ 0.3694	44.00	$ 16.25
Veggie Trails Jerky (veg)		$ 1.71	12.00	$ 20.52
Pekara Cookie/Brownie		$ 1.06	5.00	$ 5.30
Squigglies (Individual)	30 per box	$ 0.81	9.00	$ 7.29
Red Vine	Quantity Per Box	15.00		
	Case	$ 7.495	2.00	$ 14.99
	Individual Boxes	$ 0.50	3.00	$ 1.50
Popcorn:				
Bags of Popcorn		$ 18.69	4.00	$ 74.76
Popcorn Oil boxes		$ 45.31	3.00	$ 135.93
Popcorn Salt boxes		$ 1.81	1.25	$ 2.26
Butter Topping (case)		$ 39.33	1.50	$ 59.00
Total Candy & Snack Inventory				$ 2,020.50
Alcoholic Beverages				
Beers:				
Boddingtons Pub Ale	Quantity Per Box	24.00		
	Case	$ 43.84	6.00	$ 263.04
	Individual Beers	$ 1.8267	9.00	$ 16.44
Heineken	Quantity Per Box	24.00		
	Case	$ 31.54	5.00	$ 157.70
	Individual Beers	$ 1.3142	16.00	$ 21.03
Guinness	Quantity Per Box	24.00		
	Case	$ 43.24	3.00	$ 129.72
	Individual Beers	$ 1.8017	7.00	$ 12.61
Bud Light	Quantity Per Box	24.00		
	Case	$ 21.21	1.50	$ 31.81
	Individual Beers	$ 1.13	7.00	$ 7.92
Miller Lite	Quantity Per Box	24.00		
	Case	$ 22.06	1.25	$ 27.57
	Individual Beers	$ 0.9192	16.00	$ 14.71
Wines				
Silver Point Pinot Noir	Bottle	$ 9.35	5.00	$ 46.75
Maryhill "Winemakers Red"	Bottle	$ 9.49	4.00	$ 37.96
Coopers Creek Sauvignon Blanc	Bottle	$ 10.85	3.00	$ 32.55
Coopers Creek Chardonnay	Bottle	$ 10.86	8.00	$ 86.88
Yali Sauvignon Blanc	Bottle	$ 10.03	4.00	$ 40.12

Exhibit 4.3: Physical Count of Concession Stand as of 11/30 (cont'd)

(Alcoholic Beverages cont'd.)		Unit Price	Quantity In Stock	Value as of 11/30
Alcohol:				
Bailey's Irish Cream	Bottle	$ 33.44	3.00	$ 100.32
Godiva Chocolate Liqueur	Bottle	$ 30.68	2.00	$ 61.36
Oban Scotch	Bottle	$ 65.65	1.50	$ 98.48
Buffalo Trace Bourbon	Bottle	$ 28.06	3.00	$ 84.18
Rokk Vodka	Bottle	$ 15.93	2.00	$ 31.86
Captain Morgan's Rum	Bottle	$ 25.93	4.00	$ 103.72
Total Alcoholic Beverage Inventory				$ 1,406.73
Non-Alcoholic Beverages				
Soda:				
Pepsi		$ 73.67	2.25	$ 165.76
Cherry Pepsi		$ 45.65	3.00	$ 136.95
Sierra Mist		$ 45.65	2.00	$ 91.30
Root Beer		$ 47.94	2.50	$ 119.85
Diet Pepsi (reg)		$ 73.67	3.00	$ 221.01
Diet Pepsi (caffeine free)		$ 47.94	1.00	$ 47.94
Lemonade		$ 73.67	3.00	$ 221.01
Mountain Dew		$ 73.67	3.00	$ 221.01
CO2 tanks		$ 23.48	2.00	$ 46.96
Coffee, Tea, Hot Chocolate:				
Boxes of Hot Chocolate	Quantity Per Box	42.00		
	Box	$ 12.04	2.00	$ 24.08
	Individual Envelope	$ 0.2867	8.00	$ 2.29
Swiss Miss (box of 60)		$ 7.28	1.00	$ 7.28
Boxes of Tea	Quantity Per Box	18.00		
	Box	$ 2.71	1.00	$ 2.71
	Bag	$ 0.1506	14.00	$ 2.11
2 lb. bags of coffee		$ 27.74	3.00	$ 83.22
Iced Tea - Gallon brew packs		$ 1.06	2.00	$ 2.12
Coffee cream - box		$ 13.95	1.25	$ 17.44
Juice, Waters:				
Red Bull (reg. and diet)	Quantity Per Box	24.00		
	Case	$ 34.05	1.75	$ 59.59
	Can	$ 1.4188	9.00	$ 12.77
Cranberry & Grapefruit Juice	Quantity Per Box	12.00		
	Case	$ 18.53	0.75	$ 13.90
	Bottle	$ 1.54	8.00	$ 12.35

Exhibit 4.3: Physical Count of Concession Stand as of 11/30 (cont'd)

(Non-Alcoholic Beverages cont'd.)		Unit Price	Quantity In Stock	Value as of 11/30
Fuze	Quantity Per Box	12.00		
	Case	$ 11.94	0.75	$ 8.96
	Bottle	$ 0.99	11.00	$ 10.89
Vitamin Water (reg. and diet)	Quantity Per Box	15.00		
	Case	$ 13.05	1.00	$ 13.05
	Bottle	$ 0.87	14.00	$ 12.18
Bottled Water	Quantity Per Box	35.00		
	Case	$ 4.00	2.00	$ 8.00
	Bottle	$ 0.1143	12.00	$ 1.37
	Quantity Per Box	12.00		
Sobe Water	Case	$ 13.05	3.00	$ 39.15
Total Non-Alcoholic Beverages				**$ 1,605.25**
Concession Supplies:				
Paper goods:				
Napkins - 4 pack		$ 10.03	2.00	$ 20.06
Paper Towels - 16 pack box		$ 25.00	3.00	$ 75.00
Straws (case)		$ 17.97	2.00	$ 35.94
Coffee Stirrers - 5000 ct box		$ 10.23	0.75	$ 7.67
Cups & Bags:				
16 oz.. soda - 20x50		$ 3.25	3.00	$ 9.75
22 oz. soda - 20x50		$ 3.36	2.00	$ 6.72
32 oz. soda - 12 x40		$ 4.92	1.00	$ 4.92
16/21 oz. soda lids - 16 x 125		$ 3.69	3.50	$ 12.92
32 oz. soda lids - 8x120		$ 3.77	3.50	$ 13.20
12 oz. hot cups - 4 sleeve pack		$ 12.44	2.25	$ 27.99
16 oz. hot cups - 4 sleeve pack		$ 13.65	2.00	$ 27.30
Hot cup lids - 500 ct. case		$ 16.76	3.00	$ 50.28
18 oz. red cups - 4 sleeve pack		$ 9.33	5.00	$ 46.65
Beer cups - 1000 box		$ 168.66	0.75	$ 126.50
Wine cups - 2000 box		$ 112.62	0.75	$ 84.47
9 oz. Water cups - 6 sleeve pack		$ 10.43	1.50	$ 15.65
Lg Popcorn bags - 500 box		$ 65.33	2.00	$ 130.66
Med Popcorn bags - 500 box		$ 55.28	1.75	$ 96.74
Small Popcorn bags - 1000 box		$ 150.72	1.25	$ 188.40
Total Concession Supplies				**$ 980.82**

Exhibit 4.3: Physical Count of Concession Stand as of 11/30 (cont'd)

	Unit Price	Quantity In Stock	Value as of 11/30
Other Supplies:			
Windex - 1 gallon	$ 11.73	2.00	$ 23.46
Simple Green - 1 gallon	$ 8.82	1.50	$ 13.23
Paper Towels (16 count)	$ 17.74	1.50	$ 26.61
Toliet Paper (24 count)	$ 18.74	4.00	$ 74.96
Rags - 350 box	$ 12.95	1.00	$ 12.95
Mop Heads - 2 pack	$ 9.81	0.50	$ 4.90
Toilet cleaner - 4 pack	$ 4.80	2.00	$ 9.60
Letterhead & Postage	$ 577.87	0.50	$ 288.94
Ticket Stock	$ 42.21	2.00	$ 84.42
Printer Ink	$ 37.00	5.00	$ 185.00
Printer Paper (case)	$ 46.23	1.75	$ 80.90
Total Concession Supplies			**$ 804.97**

SUMMARY:	
Candy & Snacks	$ 2,020.50
Alcoholic Beverages	$ 1,406.73
Non-Alcoholic Beverages	$ 1,605.25
Concession Supplies	$ 980.82
Other Supplies	$ 804.97
	$ 6,818.27

Exhibit 4.4: Movie Listing and Split Summary: 1/1 – 11/30

Feature Presentations	Ticket Sales	Distributor Split
44 Inch Chest	$ 1,962.00	$ 784.80
A Single Man	15,907.00	6,362.80
Action Replay	1,155.50	462.20
Aida	2,902.00	1,160.80
Anjaana Anjaani	1,328.50	531.40
Babies	28,298.00	11,319.20
Broken Embraces	5,630.00	2,252.00
Carmen	2,515.00	1,006.00
Catfish	14,656.50	5,862.60
City Island	6,106.00	2,442.40
Cyrus	17,236.00	6,894.40
Daybreakers	1,210.00	484.00
Departures	4,521.50	1,808.60
Fish Tank	2,473.00	989.20
Flames of Paris	1,548.50	619.40
Girl Who Played With Fire	26,699.00	10,679.60
Girl With The Dragon Tattoo	30,198.00	12,079.20
Hey Hey It's Esther Blueburger	336.00	134.40
I Am Love	6,308.00	2,523.20
Khatta Meetha	827.50	331.00
Khelein	758.00	303.20
Love's Labour's Lost	815.00	326.00
Mao's Last Dancer	7,299.00	2,919.60
Me and Orson Welles	7,379.00	2,951.60
Metropolis	4,328.00	1,731.20
Mid-August Lunch	10,223.00	4,089.20
Millenium - The Story Documentary	353.50	141.40
Mother and Child	3,781.00	1,512.40
New Art Film Festival	3,803.00	1,521.20
Oscar Shorts 2010	6,672.00	2,668.80
Restrepo	6,969.00	2,787.60
Revolting	1,455.00	582.00
Secret in Their Eyes	16,917.00	6,766.80
Solitary Man	6,670.00	*2,668.00
Some Like It Hot	2,953.00	1,181.20
South of the Border	4,957.00	1,982.80
Takedowns and Falls	644.00	257.60
Tamara Drewe	5,395.00	2,158.00
Tees Maar Khan	748.00	299.20
The Art of the Steal	5,009.00	2,003.60
The Extra Man	1,628.00	651.20
The Last Station	12,863.00	5,145.20
The Messenger	6,948.00	2,779.20

Feature Presentations (cont'd)	Ticket Sales	Distributor Split
The White Ribbon	11,056.00	4,422.40
Waiting for Superman	10,057.00	4,022.80
Winter's Bone	6,579.50	2,631.80
Total Feature Presentations	$ 318,078.00	$ 127,231.20

Midnight Movies	Ticket Sales	Distributor Split
12 Monkeys	$ 805.00	$ 322.00
28 Days Later	115.00	46.00
8 Mile	100.00	40.00
Akira	825.00	330.00
Better Off Dead	1,135.00	454.00
Black Dynamite	1,455.00	582.00
Candyman	500.00	200.00
Donnie Darko	555.00	222.00
Drag Me to Hell	895.00	358.00
Duke of Uke Live	300.00	120.00
Evil Dead	3,665.00	1,466.00
Ferris Bueller	305.00	*122.00
Get Him to the Greek	780.00	312.00
Harold and Kumar	405.00	162.00
Hedwig and the Angry Inch	1,585.00	634.00
High Fidelity	2,070.00	828.00
Hot Fuzz	1,575.00	630.00
HouseFull	745.00	298.00
Imaginarium of Dr Parnassus	2,175.00	870.00
Karthik Calling Karthik	1,035.00	414.00
Kick-Ass	1,395.00	558.00
Leading Ladies	565.00	226.00
Legend of Drunken Master	1,350.00	540.00
Let the Right One In	1,690.00	676.00
Life of Brian	1,915.00	*766.00
Mayabazaar	345.00	138.00
Natural Born Killers	910.00	364.00
Old School	850.00	340.00
Paranormal Activity	755.00	302.00
Planes, Trains, and Automobiles	770.00	308.00
Pulp Fiction	1,865.00	746.00
Rattle and Hum	285.00	114.00
Reservoir Dogs	840.00	336.00
Runaways	1,915.00	766.00
Secret of Kells	8,795.00	3,518.00
Sexy Beast	260.00	104.00
Shaun of the Dead	2,685.00	1,074.00
Shine a Light	320.00	128.00
Shutter Island	1,445.00	578.00
Splice	865.00	346.00
Superbad	450.00	180.00

Midnight Movies (cont'd)	Ticket Sales	Distributor Split
The Cell	745.00	298.00
The Crazies	995.00	398.00
The Descent	865.00	346.00
The Last Waltz	1,290.00	516.00
The Room	9,225.00	3,690.00
The Thing	1,465.00	586.00
Winnebago Man	2,765.00	1,106.00
Zombieland	2,600.00	1,040.00
Total Midnight Movies	$ 71,245.00	$ 28,498.00
Grand Total	$ 389,323.00	$ 155,729.20
* Split unpaid as of 11/30.		$3,556.00

Exhibit 4.5: Summary of December 2010 Transactions & Events

Wednesday, December 1:

i. Dropped off a $674.12 loan payment (check # 2122) at NCH Bank ($261.21 is principal with the remaining balance being interest).
ii. Met with the owner of the Cherry Street Coffee House to discuss a cross-promotion and an on screen advertising ("OSA") contract.

Friday, December 3:

i. Received two $500 payments in the mail representing amounts due for November OSA.
ii. Purchased office supplies at Staples. Paid $145 (charged to corporate credit card).
iii. Both Carlos and Mr. Howell were interviewed by the local news station for a special broadcast covering the 100-year anniversary of the theater. During the interview, they were honored to learn that they had been chosen by the city of Seattle to be the "Grand Marshalls" for the upcoming holiday Parade of Lights. This well-loved Seattle tradition draws hundreds of families to the downtown area. The highlight of this event is the final float which, of course, carries Santa Claus. This year, Santa will be "going to the movies," and will ride a float with a replica of The Park Cinema marquee. Carlos and Martin will follow in a horse-drawn carriage.
iv. Recognizing the anniversary and parade as a valuable marketing opportunity, Carlos met with the sales manager at the *Seattle Times* and purchased advertising to run the same weekend as the parade.
v. In preparation for the parade, Carlos ordered customized balloons and refrigerator magnets to hand out to the crowd. The promotional items contain the business name and a new logo celebrating the 100-year anniversary. Vendor: Precision Graphics, list price $1,025. Payment terms of 1/10, n/30. Carlos chose the more expensive, expedited shipping option for an additional cost of $75. The goods will be shipped (FOB shipping point, freight prepaid) and are guaranteed to arrive no later than Friday, December 10.[1]

Saturday, December 4:

Paid bills:

a. Paid a contractor $1,200 for electrical work, plaster and ceiling repair (check #2123).
b. Paid Premier Entertainment $500 for November fees plus $3,556 for Premier's share ("split") of November ticket sales (check #2124).
c. Paid Northwest Supply $2,775 for November purchases (check #2125).
d. Paid $3,899 (on corporate credit card) for November purchases (check #2127). Voided check #2126.

---

[1] For purposes of the discount, assume that the 10-day period begins at the time of title transfer, and the discount applies to the merchandise only (and not the shipping charge).

Monday, December 6:

i. Susan from Touchdown Entertainment stopped by and paid its $1,500 outstanding account balance. This payment represented the balance due for its October and November, 2010 theater rentals. She signed a rental contract locking in dates for February and April 2011 events and made a deposit totaling $600.
ii. Met with various local insurance agents to get bids on the building and liquor liability insurance policies. The existing building insurance coverage expires in December of 2010 and the liquor liability expires in June of 2011.

Thursday, December 9:

i. Received an email from Precision Graphics indicating that the promotional items ordered on December 3 were shipped.
ii. Received a panicked phone call from the Seattle Model's Guild hoping to move a private event scheduled for the following day to The Park. Due to the short time frame, no deposit was made.
iii. Bought an admission pass for Carlos to attend the Minneapolis Underground Film festival to be held later in the month. Made hotel reservations and booked flights charging everything to the corporate credit card.
   - Airfare $325
   - Film Festival 3-day platinum VIP pass $525.

Friday, December 10:

i. Received a bill from Northwest Supply for concession purchases delivered on December 6 (*Exhibit 4.6a*).[2]
ii. The promotional balloons and refrigerator magnets were delivered. The shipment included an invoice detailing a total amount owed of $1,100 after a prepaid shipping cost of $75. Payment terms of 1/10, n/30.
iii. The Seattle Model's Guild's private event was held from 1:00-4:00 p.m. Before leaving, the controller paid the $600 balance in full.
iv. Met with various businesses to finalize holiday functions to be held at the theater. So far this week, The Park has received signed theater rental contracts and deposits totaling $1,200 ($900 for upcoming December events and $300 for a January rental).

Saturday, December 11:

i. Paid bills:
   a. Paid $875 for November utilities (check #2128).
   b. Paid Precision Graphics for the promotional balloons and magnets (check #2129).
   c. Paid (check #2130) for Northwest Supply invoice #7956 (*Exhibit 4.6a*).

ii. Received the payroll report (*Exhibit 4.7a*). Prepared and distributed paychecks.

[2] For purposes of the discount, assume that the 10-day period begins at the time of title transfer.

Sunday, December 12:

The holiday parade was a success! We came home empty-handed with not a single promotional balloon or magnet remaining.

Monday, December 13:

i. Tracy faxed over the Box Office Summary sheet for *Solitary Man*, the feature movie closing on 12/11 (*Exhibit 4.8a*). She also provided the following payment summary sheet for the same period:

Figure 4.3

PAYMENT SUMMARY SHEET:

12/1-12/11/2010	Reported per Register System				
	Cash	Debit Card	Credit Card	Loyalty Card	Grand Total
Box Office Ticket Sales	$1,814.84	$2,441.62	$4,661.64	$181.90	$9,100.00
*Loyalty Card Sales	$150.00	$350.00	$100.00	N/A	$600.00
**Concession Sales	$1,457.19	$1,960.50	$3,742.97	$146.05	$7,306.71
**Sales Tax Collected	$138.43	$186.25	$355.58	$13.88	$694.14
	$3,560.46	$4,938.37	$8,860.19	$341.83	$17,700.85

Cash collected per register system	$ 3,560.46
Plus: Beginning cash in register drawer	$ 2,100.00
Expected ending register drawer cash	$ 5,660.46
Cash Over / (Short)	4.00
Cash counted in register	$ 5,664.46
Less: Beginning cash in register drawer	$(2,100.00)
Equals: Expected bank deposits (12/1-12/11)	$ 3,564.46

*As discussed in the ***Narrative***, each $50 loyalty card purchased was loaded with an additional $5 "loyalty premium" (not included in *Figure 4.3*). This premium, when combined with the initial $50 purchase, gives the patron $55 to actually spend at the theater.

**The Concession Sales line item represents the concession sales only and does not include sales tax collected. The Sales Tax Collected line item represents the 9.5% sales tax The Park collects upfront from the customer at the time of sale (concession sales only). It is obligated to remit the proceeds to the state-taxing authority on a monthly basis.

ii. Paid Premier Entertainment its share of ticket proceeds for the three movies shown from 12/1 to 12/11 (*Exhibit 4.8a*) (check #2140).

Wednesday, December 15:

i. Charged $1,062.72 of liquor purchases for the concession to the corporate credit card.
ii. Received a phone call from the sales manager at KPLZ radio indicating that we had expended the entire $3,500 advance payment made in October 2010 for advertising spots. In order to keep the advertisements running without interruption, KPLZ required another $3,500 payment by the end of the week.

iii. In anticipation of being out of town to attend the film festival over the weekend, Carlos stopped by mid-week and paid the following bills:

   a. An invoice from *Seattle Times* for the parade of lights advertisement and for some smaller advertisements that will run the first week of January. Paid $2,650 in total (check #2141), of which $1600 was for the parade advertising.
   b. The first quarter 2011 building rent (check #2142).

On his way home, Carlos dropped a $3,500 payment (check #2143) off at KPLZ radio and withdrew $500 from the theater's bank account to cover incidentals on the trip.

Tuesday, December 21:

i. Met with Martin Howell about the proposed stock purchase and the need to upgrade the theater to a digital projection system that is industry-compliant and 3D capable. Reviewed available projector systems online.
ii. Ordered a new digital projector system and screen that is industry-compliant and also 3D capable. Vendor: Digital Projection from Oxford, OH. List price $52,500. Negotiated a trade discount of 3% and payment terms of 2/10, n/30.[3] Shipment (FOB destination) has been promised to take place no later than December 26.
iii. Received invoice #8025 from Northwest Supply (*Exhibit 4.6b*) in the mail.
iv. Renewed the building liability insurance policy expiring 12/31/10. The new policy is effective 1/1/2011 and covers a 9-month period. The $3,465 premium was paid in full (check #2144).
v. Paid $3,250 (check #2145) to sponsor two little league teams. The team jerseys will have the theater name and logo. The season starts in May and finishes at the end of June.

Thursday, December 23:

i. Paid the accounting firm $160 for its December services (check #2146).
ii. Charged $1,601.14 of liquor purchases for the concession to the corporate credit card.
iii. Wrote the following checks to local charities:

[3] For purposes of the discount, assume that the 10-day period begins at the time of title transfer, and the discount applies to the merchandise only (and not the shipping charge).

West Seattle Youth Arts Program	$500 (#2147)
Seattle Conservatory of Music	$500 (#2148)
Seattle Youth Recreation Club	$500 (#2149)

Monday, December 27:

i. Received the payroll report (*Exhibit 4.7b*). Prepared and distributed paychecks.
ii. Carlos paid himself $2,500 (check #2159) for his December dividend. After a brief phone call to the tax accountant, it was determined that a December dividend should not be paid. Check #2159 was voided.
iii. Purchased $120 of office supplies at Office Depot (charged to corporate credit card).
iv. Tracy faxed over the Box Office Summary sheet for *127 Hours*, the feature movie closing on 12/25 (*Exhibit 4.8b*). She also provided the following payment summary sheet for the same period:

Figure 4.4

PAYMENT SUMMARY SHEET:

12/12-12/25/2010	Reported per Register System				
	Cash	Debit Card	Credit Card	Loyalty Card	Grand Total
Box Office Ticket Sales	$2,784.95	$3,630.73	$6,815.06	$283.76	$13,514.50
* Loyalty Card Sales	$150.00	$250.00	$300.00	N/A	$700.00
**Concession Sales	$2,236.11	$2,915.21	$5,471.90	$225.54	$10,848.76
**Sales Tax Collected	$212.43	$276.95	$519.83	$21.43	$1,030.64
	$5,383.49	$7,072.89	$13,106.79	$530.73	$26,093.90

Cash collected per register system	$ 5,383.49
Plus: Beginning cash in register drawer	$ 2,100.00
Expected ending register drawer cash	$ 7,483.49
Cash Over / (Short)	(16.82)
Cash counted in register	$ 7,466.67
Less: Beginning cash in register drawer	$(2,100.00)
Equals: Expected bank deposits (12/12-12/25)	$ 5,366.67

* As discussed in the ***Narrative***, each $50 loyalty card purchased was loaded with an additional $5 "loyalty premium" (not included in *Figure 4.4*). This premium, when combined with the initial $50 purchase, gives the patron $55 to actually spend at the theater.

**The Concession Sales line item represents the concession sales only and does not include sales tax collected. The Sales Tax Collected line item represents the 9.5% sales tax The Park collects upfront from the customer at the time of sale (concession sales only). It is obligated to remit the proceeds to the state-taxing authority on a monthly basis.

Thursday, December 30:

i. Received an email from Digital Projection indicating that the new digital projector system had been shipped and is expected to arrive within 3-6 days.

ii. Paid invoice #8025 (check #2160) from Northwest Supply (*Exhibit 4.6b*).[4]

iii. Matt is taking a few days off to spend with his wife and new son. After talking to Tracy, Carlos formally notified Matt that he would be paid a $1,500 bonus (when he returns to work) in recognition of his excellent effort over the last year. Carlos also decided to approach Pete Shkumatov about becoming an assistant manager. The promotion (if accepted) would increase his pay to $10 per hour.

iv. Received $3,000 of OSA payments in the mail. $1,500 of the amount paid was for December 2010 OSA, with the remaining $1,500 being paid in advance by OSA customer Zanadu Comics toward its January, February, and March 2011 OSA. Carlos mailed bills totaling $1,000 for the remaining amounts owed for the December OSA:

Total December OSA contracts	$2,500.00
Payments already received	(1,500.00)
Balance still owed	$1,000.00

v. Charged $614.18 of liquor purchases for the concession to the corporate credit card.

[4] For purposes of the discount, assume that the 10-day period begins at the time of title transfer.

Exhibit 4.6a: Northwest Concession Supply Invoice (12/6)

Northwest Concession Supply, Inc
Over 75 years serving the greater Seattle area.

3801 S. Graham Street
Seattle, Washington 98118
Phone 1-800-999-2415 Fax 1-800-999-2416

INVOICE

INVOICE #7956
DATE: 12/6/2010

TO:
The Park Cinema
415 Cedar Street
Seattle, Washington
98121

FOR:
Concession Deliveries on 12/6

TERMS:
FOB Shipping Point
2/10, n/30

DESCRIPTION	AMOUNT
Candy & Snack Concession Items	$621.77
Non-Alcoholic Beverage Concession Items	827.61
Concession Supplies	148.62
TOTAL	$1,598.00

Make all checks payable to NWCS, Inc.

Thank you for your business!

Exhibit 4.6b: Northwest Concession Supply Invoice (12/17)

Northwest Concession Supply, Inc
Over 75 years serving the greater Seattle area.

3801 S. Graham Street
Seattle, Washington 98118
Phone 1-800-999-2415 Fax 1-800-999-2416

INVOICE

INVOICE #8025
DATE: 12/17/2010

TO:
The Park Cinema
415 Cedar Street
Seattle, Washington
98121

FOR:
Concession Deliveries on 12/17

TERMS:
FOB Shipping Point
2/10, n/30

DESCRIPTION	AMOUNT
Candy & Snack Concession Items	$466.91
Non-Alcoholic Beverage Concession Items	621.49
Concession Supplies	111.60
TOTAL	$1,200.00

Make all checks payable to NWCS, Inc.

Thank you for your business!

Exhibit 4.7a: December 11, 2010 Payroll Report

14-day pay period ending 12/11	Hourly Pay Rate	Nov. Hours	Dec. Hours	Gross Pay Nov.*	Gross Pay Dec.	Gross Pay Total	Paycheck #
Evans, Dan	$8.75	12	25	$105.00	$218.75	$323.75	#2131
Guardia, Don	$9.00		38	$0.00	$342.00	$342.00	#2132
Hart, Rick	$8.75	16	45	$140.00	$393.75	$533.75	#2133
Holtman, Kristen	$8.75		50	$0.00	$437.50	$437.50	#2134
Meijia, Luis	$9.00	18	36	$162.00	$324.00	$486.00	#2135
Moore, Heidi	$8.75	4	30	$35.00	$262.50	$297.50	#2136
Shkumatov,Pete	$8.75	14	55	$122.50	$481.25	$603.75	#2137
Tempel,Matt	$12.00	32	75	$384.00	$900.00	$1,284.00	#2138
Tsai, Will	$9.00		41	$0.00	$369.00	$369.00	#2139
		96	395	$948.50	$3,728.75	$4,677.25	

	*Nov.	Dec.	Total
Total Hours	96	395	491
Workers Comp Rate	0.45	0.45	0.45
Premiums Owed	$ 43.20	$ 177.75	$ 220.95

* Accrued at the end of November (see TN 1.1).

Exhibit 4.7b: December 25, 2010 Payroll Report

14-day pay period ending 12/25	Hourly Pay Rate	Dec. Hours	Gross Pay Total	Paycheck #
Evans, Dan	$8.75	27	$236.25	2150
Guardia, Don	$9.00	41	$369.00	2151
Hart, Rick	$8.75	48	$420.00	2152
Holtman, Kristen	$8.75	54	$472.50	2153
Meijia, Luis	$9.00	38	$342.00	2154
Moore, Heidi	$8.75	32	$280.00	2155
Shkumatov,Pete	$8.75	58	$507.50	2156
Tempel,Matt	$12.00	35	$420.00	2157
Tsai, Will	$9.00	44	$396.00	2158
		377	$3,443.25	

Total Hours	377
Workers Comp Rate	0.45
Premiums Owed	$ 169.65

Exhibit 4.8a: Box Office Summary Sheet (*Solitary Man*)

Box Office Summary Sheet

Premiere Entertainment Film Buying Service
Seattle, Washington 98103

Theatre	The Park Cinema	Feature:	**Solitary Man**
Period	12/1/10 – 12/11/10	Midnight #1:	Buried
		Midnight #2:	Easy A

	MATINEE		MIDNIGHT	FEATURE PRESENTATION				TOTAL
	Regular	Senior	Regular	Adult	Senior	Child	Student	# of Tickets
Date	$6.50	$6.00	$5.00	$9.00	$6.00	$6.00	$7.50	Total $
Wednesday				22.00	14.00		28.00	64.00
1-Dec				$198.00	$84.00		$210.00	$492.00
Thursday			32.00	21.00	18.00		24.00	95.00
2-Dec			$160.00	$189.00	$108.00		$180.00	$637.00
Friday			45.00	56.00	21.00		37.00	159.00
3-Dec			$225.00	$504.00	$126.00		$277.50	$1,132.50
Saturday	35.00	14.00	36.00	36.00	28.00		42.00	191.00
4-Dec	$227.50	$84.00	$180.00	$324.00	$168.00		$315.00	$1,298.50
Sunday	31.00	11.00		28.00	11.00		32.00	113.00
5-Dec	$201.50	$66.00		$252.00	$66.00		$240.00	$825.50
Monday				21.00	12.00		16.00	49.00
6-Dec				$189.00	$72.00		$120.00	$381.00
Tuesday				12.00	8.00		18.00	38.00
7-Dec				$108.00	$48.00		$135.00	$291.00
Wednesday				24.00	16.00		29.00	69.00
8-Dec				$216.00	$96.00		$217.50	$529.50
Thursday			16.00	36.00	18.00		41.00	111.00
9-Dec			$80.00	$324.00	$108.00		$307.50	$819.50
Friday			27.00	52.00	23.00		67.00	169.00
10-Dec			$135.00	$468.00	$138.00		$502.50	$1,243.50
Saturday	21.00	16.00	35.00	54.00	34.00		47.00	207.00
11-Dec	$136.50	$96.00	$175.00	$486.00	$204.00		$352.50	$1,450.00

Grand Total	**Matinee**	**Midnight**	**Feature**	**Total**	**Grand Total**
Ticket Count	128.00	191.00	946.00	1,265.00	**1,265.00**
$ Sales	$811.50	$955.00	$7,333.50	$9,100.00	**$9,100.00**

	S. Man	**Buried**	**Easy A**	**Total**
Ticket Count	1,074.00	113.00	78.00	1,265.00
$ Sales	$8,145.00	$565.00	$390.00	$9,100.00

Negotiated Split:	**S. Man**	**Buried**	**Easy A**	**Total**
Theater	$4,887.00	$367.25	$243.75	$5,498.00
Distributor	3,258.00	197.75	146.25	3,602.00
	$8,145.00	$565.00	$390.00	$9,100.00
Split %	40%	35%	38%	

Exhibit 4.8b: Box Office Summary Sheet (*127 Hours*)

Box Office Summary Sheet

Premiere Entertainment Film Buying Service
Seattle, Washington 98103

Theatre The Park Cinema
Period 12/12/10 12/25/10

Feature #1 **127 Hours**
Feature #2 **Nutcracker (special holiday showing, 10:00 am on Saturdays & Sundays)**
Midnight #1 Nightmare Before Christmas
Midnight #2 The Pursuit of Happyness

	MATINEE		MIDNIGHT	FEATURE PRESENTATION				TOTAL
	Regular	Senior	Regular	Adult	Senior	Child	Student	# of Tickets
Date	$6.50	$6.00	$5.00	$9.00	$6.00	$6.00	$7.50	Total $
Sunday	45.00	22.00		45.00	16.00	32.00	31.00	191.00
12-Dec	$292.50	$132.00		$405.00	$96.00	$192.00	$232.50	$1,350.00
Monday				21.00	9.00		25.00	55.00
13-Dec				$189.00	$54.00		$187.50	$430.50
Tuesday				26.00	16.00		32.00	74.00
14-Dec				$234.00	$96.00		$240.00	$570.00
Wednesday				29.00	17.00		33.00	79.00
15-Dec				$261.00	$102.00		$247.50	$610.50
Thursday			36.00	35.00	14.00		41.00	126.00
16-Dec			$180.00	$315.00	$84.00		$307.50	$886.50
Friday			45.00	46.00	23.00		42.00	156.00
17-Dec			$225.00	$414.00	$138.00		$315.00	$1,092.00
Saturday	44.00	22.00	28.00	57.00	26.00	48.00	76.00	301.00
18-Dec	$286.00	$132.00	$140.00	$513.00	$156.00	$288.00	$570.00	$2,085.00
Sunday	49.00	31.00		31.00	16.00	56.00	32.00	215.00
19-Dec	$318.50	$186.00		$279.00	$96.00	$336.00	$240.00	$1,455.50
Monday				24.00	0.00		18.00	42.00
20-Dec				$216.00	$0.00		$135.00	$351.00
Tuesday				37.00	6.00		21.00	64.00
21-Dec				$333.00	$36.00		$157.50	$526.50
Wednesday				44.00	14.00		22.00	80.00
22-Dec				$396.00	$84.00		$165.00	$645.00
Thursday			16.00	48.00	21.00		43.00	128.00
23-Dec			$80.00	$432.00	$126.00		$322.50	$960.50
Friday			14.00	56.00	26.00		48.00	144.00
24-Dec			$70.00	$504.00	$156.00		$360.00	$1,090.00
Saturday	11.00	7.00	32.00	63.00	31.00		58.00	202.00
25-Dec	$71.50	$42.00	$160.00	$567.00	$186.00		$435.00	$1,461.50

Grand Total	Matinee	Midnight	Feature	Total	Grand Total
Ticket Count	231.00	171.00	1,455.00	1,857.00	**1,857.00**
$ Sales	$1,460.50	$855.00	$11,199.00	$13,514.50	**$13,514.50**

	127 Hrs	Nutcracker	Nightmare	Pursuit	Total
Ticket Count	1,150.00	536.00	109.00	62.00	1,857.00
$ Sales	$8,743.50	$3,916.00	$545.00	$310.00	$13,514.50

Negotiated Split:	127 Hrs	Nutcracker	Nightmare	Pursuit	Total
Theater	$5,071.23	$2,153.80	$359.70	$213.90	$7,798.63
Distributor	3,672.27	1,762.20	185.30	96.10	5,715.87
	$8,743.50	$3,916.00	$545.00	$310.00	$13,514.50
Split %	42%	45%	34%	31%	

Exhibit 4.9: Summary of January 2011 Events

Saturday, January 1:

Counted supplies and other verifiable assets noting the following quantities:

Concession:

Candy & Snacks	$1,474.74	
Alcoholic Beverages	$1,254.78	
Non-Alcoholic Beverages	$1,474.69	
Concession Supplies	$1,001.66	
Total		$5,205.87
Other Supplies		$ 541.36
Grand Total		$5,747.23

Monday, January 3:

i. The new digital projector system ordered on December 21 (*Exhibit 4.5*) was delivered. Ideally, the old system will be removed and this system will be installed and operating by late January.
ii. Received invoice #8165 from Northwest Supply (*Exhibit 4.10*) in the mail.
iii. Paid $500 (check #2161) to Premiere Entertainment for its December consulting fee as well as its portion of the ticket proceeds for *127 Hours* (which closed on December 25; *Exhibit 4.8b*).

Wednesday, January 5:

i. Talked to the owner of Cherry Street Café about December's cross promotion. Under this promotion, The Park patrons could bring a theater ticket stub to the café and receive a free dessert for each full price dessert purchased. Each business also will also display advertising and promotional items for the other business. We agreed to share the cost of the free desserts evenly. During the month of December, 44 "free" desserts were given out for a total cost of $275. Paid check #2162.
ii. Mailed billing statement for various corporate events held at The Park in December:

Total amount owed for December theater rental	$3,500.00
Less: advance deposit made	(900.00)
Balance due	$2,600.00

Saturday, January 8:

i. Received the payroll report (*Exhibit 4.11*). Prepared and distributed paychecks.
ii. Received $500 in the mail representing amounts owed for December OSA. Contacted the owner of Shameless, a downtown clothing boutique, about the $500 remaining balance owed for December OSA. Discovered the shop had closed in late December and the

owner had left the community. We intend to collect the full balance owed and have asked our attorney to locate a forwarding address.

Monday, January 10:

i. Paid $1,331.39 representing the total amount owed for the fourth quarter 2010 workers' compensation insurance premium (check #2172).
ii. The evening news television broadcast covering The Park's 100-year anniversary aired.
iii. A box containing 2,500 concession napkins was delivered featuring the new 100-year anniversary logo. The box included an invoice (*Exhibit 4.12*).
iv. The December bank statement was received in the mail.

- Students who will not be required to complete ***Case 4-4*** should incorporate *Exhibit TN 4.3* here and prepare all entries that should be made as a result of the information provided in this exhibit.
- Students who will be required to complete ***Case 4-4*** should move on with the problem. All entries that should be made as a result of reconciling the December bank statement will be recorded in ***Case 4-4***.

v. Received a schedule in the mail detailing the interest and principal breakdown for the payments made on the start-up loan taken out in 2009 (*Exhibit 4.13*). After comparing this statement to *Exhibit TN 4.2*, you quickly note that the interest and principal on the loan had not been properly accounted for during the year. In anticipation of making an adjusting entry, you reviewed the 2010 general ledger activity and prepared the following summary detailing the account activity:

Figure 4.5

	Loan Balance	Interest Expense	Interest Payable
12/31/2009	73,559.41	0.00	429.10
Jan. 1 payment	-245.02	0.00	-429.10
Feb. 1-Nov. 30 payments	-6,741.20	0.00	0.00
December 1 payment	-261.21	412.91	0.00
12/31/2010 UTB (*Exhibit TN 4.2*)	66,311.98	412.91	0.00

vi. After discovering the error with the loan interest (item v), you did a little investigating and determined that $575 of interest income (earned on the bank account balance between January 1 and November 30, 2010) had been erroneously credited to "Miscellaneous Expense!" Concerned over Matt's qualifications to handle the books, you made a mental note to talk to Tracy, hopeful that she and Carlos would hire you to handle the weekly accounting.
vii. Tracy faxed over the Box Office Summary sheet for *The Girl Who Kicked the Hornets' Nest*, the feature movie closing on 1/8 (*Exhibit 4.14*). She also provided the following payment summary sheet for the same period:

Figure 4.6

Payment Summary 12/26/2010 - 1/8/2011	Reported per Register System						
	Cash	Debit Card	Credit Card	Loyalty Card	Grand Total	+Cash counted in Drawer	Cash Over or (Short)
Ticket Sales							
12/26-12/31	$1,538.36	$1,805.00	$3,216.30	$134.34	$6,694.00		
1/1-1/8	$1,806.31	$2,119.41	$3,776.54	$157.74	$7,860.00		
Total	$3,344.67	$3,924.41	$6,992.84	$292.08	$14,554.00		
*Loyalty Card Sales							
12/26-12/31	$50.00	$50.00	$100.00	N/A	$200.00		
1/1-1/8	$250.00	$50.00	$100.00	N/A	$400.00		
Total	$300.00	$100.00	$200.00		$600.00		
**Concession Sales							
12/26-12/31	$1,235.20	$1,449.12	$2,582.48	$107.85	$5,374.65		
1/1-1/8	$1,445.11	$1,695.38	$3,021.34	$126.18	$6,288.01		
Total	$2,680.31	$3,144.50	$5,603.82	$234.03	$11,662.66		
**Sales Tax Collected							
12/26-12/31	$117.34	$137.67	$245.34	$10.25	$510.60		
1/1-1/8	$137.29	$161.06	$287.03	$11.99	$597.37		
Total	$254.63	$298.73	$532.37	$22.24	$1,107.97		
Grand Total							
12/26-12/31	$2,940.90	$3,441.79	$6,144.12	$252.44	$12,779.25	$2,946.40	$5.50
1/1-1/8	$3,638.71	$4,025.85	$7,184.91	$295.91	$15,145.38	$3,631.21	($7.50)
Total	$6,579.61	$7,467.64	$13,329.03	$548.35	$27,924.63	$6,577.61	($2.00)

* As discussed in the ***Narrative***, each $50 loyalty card purchased was loaded with an additional $5 "loyalty premium" (not included in *Figure 4.6*). This premium, when combined with the initial $50 purchase, gives the patron $55 to actually spend at the theater.

**The Concession Sales line item represents the concession sales only and does not include sales tax collected. The Sales Tax Collected line item represents the 9.5% sales tax The Park collects upfront from the customer at the time of sale (concession sales only). It is obligated to remit the proceeds to the state-taxing authority on a monthly basis.

+This count does not include the $2,100 of the beginning register drawer cash.

Wednesday, January 12:

i. Three new corporate events were booked as a result of the television broadcast. Contracts were signed and deposits totaling $1,200 were collected.

ii. Received a year-end statement from KPLZ radio noting that of the 35 radio spots purchased on 12/15 (*Exhibit 4.5*), 19 had run as of 12/31.

iii. Received an email from an Edison Advertising sales representative wanting to set up a meeting to renew the LED billboard lease. Carlos believes that this form of advertising has been too expensive (he paid $5,500 on August 1, 2010 for six months of rental expiring January 31, 2011). Further, given the location of the billboards, he does not intend to renew the contract.

iv. Received the year-end depreciation schedule from the outside accounting firm. Reviewed it noting no differences from the schedule mailed in November (*Exhibit 4.2*).

Saturday, January 15:

Paid bills:

a. Paid the December utilities $885 (check #2173).
b. Paid the $185 phone bill for December (check #2174).
c. Paid the monthly corporate credit card bill in full (check #2175) (see *Exhibit 4.15*).
d. Paid (check #2176) to Premier Entertainment for its share of ticket sales for *The Girl Who Kicked the Hornets' Nest* (*Exhibit 4.14*).
e. Paid for the concession napkins received on 1/10 (check #2177).
f. Paid (check #2178) Northwest Supply invoice #8165 (*Exhibit 4.10*).
g. Paid Pro Quality Office Cleaning $325 for December cleaning services (check #2179).
h. Paid $2,235.38 to the state-taxing authority (check #2180) representing amounts owed for December sales tax.

Exhibit 4.10: Northwest Concession Supply Invoice (12/31)

Northwest Concession Supply, Inc
Over 75 years serving the greater Seattle area.

3801 S. Graham Street
Seattle, Washington 98118
Phone 1-800-999-2415 Fax 1-800-999-2416

INVOICE

INVOICE #8165
DATE: 12/31/2010

TO:
The Park Cinema
415 Cedar Street
Seattle, Washington
98121

FOR:
Concession Deliveries on 12/31

TERMS:
FOB Shipping Point
2/10, n/30

DESCRIPTION	AMOUNT
Candy & Snack Concession Items	$777.02
Non-Alcoholic Beverage Concession Items	1,034.25
Concession Supplies	185.73
TOTAL	$1,997.00

Make all checks payable to NWCS, Inc.

Thank you for your business!

Exhibit 4.11: January 2011 Payroll Report

14-day pay period ending 1/8	Hourly Pay Rate	Dec. Hours	Jan. Hours	Gross Pay Dec.	Gross Pay Jan.	Gross Pay Total	Paycheck #
Evans, Dan	$8.75	16	24	$140.00	$210.00	$350.00	#2163
Guardia, Don	$9.00	8	32	$72.00	$288.00	$360.00	#2164
Hart, Rick	$8.75	32	28	$280.00	$245.00	$525.00	#2165
Holtman, Kristen	$8.75		16	$0.00	$140.00	$140.00	#2166
Meijia, Luis	$9.00	24	36	$216.00	$324.00	$540.00	#2167
Moore, Heidi	$8.75	16	20	$140.00	$175.00	$315.00	#2168
Shkumatov, Pete	$8.75	32	52	$280.00	$455.00	$735.00	#2169
Tempel, Matt	$12.00	35	66	$420.00	$792.00	$1,212.00	#2170
Tempel, Matt	2010 Bonus			$1,500.00	$0.00	$1,500.00	#2171
Tsai, Will	$9.00			$0.00	$0.00	$0.00	
		163	274	$3,048.00	$2,629.00	$5,677.00	

	December	January	Total
Total Hours	163	274	437
Workers' Comp Rate	0.45	0.45	0.45
Premiums Owed	73.35	123.30	196.65

Exhibit 4.12: Kardwell Custom Design Invoice

KARDWELL CUSTOM DESIGN

INVOICE

BILL TO	SHIP TO
The Park Cinema 415 Cedar Street Seattle, Washington 98121	The Park Cinema 415 Cedar Street Seattle, Washington 98121

Invoice #	79876
Invoice Date	12/30/2010
Customer ID	Park456

DATE	YOUR ORDER #	OUR ORDER #	SALES REP.	F.O.B.	SHIP DATE	SHIPPING TIME	PMT. TERMS
12/13	phone	25679	Jason	Shipping point	12/30	12:05 p.m.	1/10, n/30

QTY	ITEM	UNITS	DESCRIPTION	DISCOUNT %	TAXABLE	UNIT PRICE	TOTAL
2,500			Custom logo napkins			.11	275.00
						Subtotal	
						Tax	
						Shipping	15.00
						Miscellaneous	
						BALANCE DUE	290.00

Please return the portion below with your payment.

REMITTANCE

Invoice #	
Customer ID	
Date	
Amount Enclosed	

Exhibit 4.13: Start-up Loan Amortization Schedule*

Payment Date	Payment	Interest	Principal	Balance
				$75,000.00
1-Jul-09	$674.12	437.50	(236.62)	$74,763.38
1-Aug-09	$674.12	436.12	(238.00)	$74,525.38
1-Sep-09	$674.12	434.73	(239.39)	$74,285.99
1-Oct-09	$674.12	433.33	(240.79)	$74,045.20
1-Nov-09	$674.12	431.93	(242.19)	$73,803.01
1-Dec-09	$674.12	430.52	(243.60)	$73,559.41
1-Jan-10	$674.12	429.10	(245.02)	$73,314.39
1-Feb-10	$674.12	427.67	(246.45)	$73,067.94
1-Mar-10	$674.12	426.23	(247.89)	$72,820.05
1-Apr-10	$674.12	424.78	(249.34)	$72,570.71
1-May-10	$674.12	423.33	(250.79)	$72,319.92
1-Jun-10	$674.12	421.87	(252.25)	$72,067.67
1-Jul-10	$674.12	420.39	(253.73)	$71,813.94
1-Aug-10	$674.12	418.91	(255.21)	$71,558.73
1-Sep-10	$674.12	417.43	(256.69)	$71,302.04
1-Oct-10	$674.12	415.93	(258.19)	$71,043.85
1-Nov-10	$674.12	414.42	(259.70)	$70,784.15
1-Dec-10	$674.12	412.91	(261.21)	$70,522.94
1-Jan-11	$674.12	411.38	(262.74)	$70,260.20
1-Feb-11	$674.12	409.85	(264.27)	$69,995.93
1-Mar-11	$674.12	408.31	(265.81)	$69,730.12
1-Apr-11	$674.12	406.76	(267.36)	$69,462.76
1-May-11	$674.12	405.20	(268.92)	$69,193.84
1-Jun-11	$674.12	403.63	(270.49)	$68,923.35
1-Jul-11	$674.12	402.05	(272.07)	$68,651.28

* It should be assumed that the above amortization schedule which was provided by the bank is accurate and does not contain errors.

Exhibit 4.14: Box Office Summary Sheet (*The Girl Who Kicked the Hornets' Nest*)

Box Office Summary Sheet

Premiere Entertainment Film Buying Service
Seattle Washington, 98103

Theatre: The Park Cinema
Period: 12/26/10 – 1/8/11

Feature #1: The Girl Who Kicked the Hornets' Nest
Midnight: High Fidelity 12/30-1/1
Midnight: Repeat Performance 1/6-1/8

	MATINEE		MIDNIGHT	FEATURE PRESENTATION				TOTAL
	Regular	Senior	Regular	Adult	Senior	Child	Student	# of Tickets
Date	$6.50	$6.00	$5.00	$9.00	$6.00	$6.00	$7.50	Total $
Sunday	72	38		65	22		52	249
26-Dec	$468.00	$228.00		$585.00	$132.00		$390.00	$1,803.00
Monday				32	14		46	92
27-Dec				$288.00	$84.00		$345.00	$717.00
Tuesday				29	14		77	120
28-Dec				$261.00	$84.00		$577.50	$922.50
Wednesday				17	11		32	60
29-Dec				$153.00	$66.00		$240.00	$459.00
Thursday			65	28	18		41	152
30-Dec			$325.00	$252.00	$108.00		$307.50	$992.50
* Friday			225	87	32		110	454
31-Dec			$1,125.00	$783.00	$192.00		$825.00	$2,925.00
Saturday	41	32	37	26	11		45	192
1-Jan	$266.50	$192.00	$185.00	$234.00	$66.00		$337.50	$1,281.00
Sunday	35	22		41	21		35	154
2-Jan	$227.50	$132.00		$369.00	$126.00		$262.50	$1,117.00
Monday				21	8		42	71
3-Jan				$189.00	$48.00		$315.00	$552.00
Tuesday				21	6		26	53
4-Jan				$189.00	$36.00		$195.00	$420.00
Wednesday				9	0		22	31
5-Jan				$81.00	$0.00		$165.00	$246.00
Thursday			37	26	8		65	136
6-Jan			$185.00	$234.00	$48.00		$487.50	$954.50
Friday			55	45	16		39	155
7-Jan			$275.00	$405.00	$96.00		$292.50	$1,068.50
Saturday	32	18	48	24	14		32	168
8-Jan	$208.00	$108.00	$240.00	$216.00	$84.00		$240.00	$1,096.00

Grand Total	Matinee	Midnight	Feature	Total	Grand Total
Ticket Count	290.00	467.00	1,330.00	2,087.00	2,087.00
$ Sales	$1,830.00	$2,335.00	$10,389.00	$14,554.00	$14,554.00

	Hornet	H. Fidelity	R. Perform.	Total
Ticket Count	1,620.00	327	140	2,087.00
$ Sales	$12,219.00	$1,635.00	$700.00	$14,554.00

Negotiated Split:	Hornet	H. Fidelity	R. Perform.	Total
Theater	$6,720.45	$1,111.80	$504.00	$8,336.25
Distributor	5,498.55	523.20	196.00	6,217.75
	$12,219.00	$1,635.00	$700.00	$14,554.00
Split %	45%	32%	28%	

* the midnight movie on 12/31 represents the first film of 2011.

Exhibit 4.15: December Corporate Credit Card Statement

Date	Vendor	Amount
12/3/2010	Staples	$ 145.00*
12/9/2010	Minneapolis Underground Film Festival	$ 525.00*
12/9/2010	Delta Airline	$ 325.00* (1)
12/12/2010	Delta Airline	$ 325.00 (2)
12/11/2010	UPS Store	$ 416.00 (3)
12/15/2010	Washington State Liquor Emporium	$1,062.72*
12/16/2010	Hyatt Regency-Minneapolis	$ 480.00 (4)
12/17/2010	Nordstrom	$ 800.00 (5)
12/17/2010	Macy's	$ 400.00 (5)
12/18/2010	Best Buy	$ 750.00 (5)
12/18/2010	Abercrombie	$ 650.00 (5)
12/23/2010	Washington State Liquor Emporium	$1,601.14*
12/27/2010	Office Depot	$ 120.00*
12/27/2010	UPS Store	$ 324.00 (3)
12/30/2010	Washington State Liquor Emporium	$ 614.18*
	Total Charges	$ 8,538.04

(1) The cost of Carlos' ticket to attend the Minneapolis Underground Film Festival (*Exhibit 4.5*, 12/9 (iii)).

(2) Tracy decided to join Carlos in Minneapolis in order to do some holiday shopping at the Mall of America.

(3) Shipping cost to return films.

(4) Due to double occupancy, the hotel rate ($160 for 3 nights) is $10 higher than originally quoted.

(5) Tracy and Carlos left town without their personal credit card. Tracy used the corporate card while holiday shopping.

* Consistent with the unadjusted "Credit Card Payable" account balance reported to you in *Exhibit TN 4.2*, these particular purchases were already recorded during the month of December.

Exhibit 4.16: The November Bank Reconciliation

(prepared by Matt Tempel, Theater Manager)

Bank Balance per 11/30 Bank Statement				$ **29,954.19**
Plus: Deposits in Transit (list individually)				
			(11/30 deposit)	**3,613.34**
Errors and other items (list individually and explain):				
Explanation				
Less: Outstanding Checks (list individually)				
	(#2076)	**Carlos Vega**	**10/18/2010**	**2,500.00**
	(#2092)	**Carlos Vega**	**11/22/2010**	**2,500.00**
	(#2112)	**Dan Evans**	**11/27/2010**	**288.75**
	(#2117)	**Heidi Moore**	**1/27/2010**	**245.00**
	(#2118)	**Pete Shkumatov**	**11/27/2010**	**586.25**
	(#2120)	**NWCS**	**11/30/2010**	**1,847.05**
Errors and other items (list individually and explain):				
Explanation				
Reconciled Balance per Bank at 11/30				$ **25,600.48**

Exhibit 4.16: The November Bank Reconciliation
(prepared by Matt Tempel, Theater Manager)

Unadjusted Balance per Checkbook at 11/30		**$ (30,686.98)**
Plus:	Interest earned during November	**128.25**
	Errors and other items (list individually and explain):	
	Explanation	
	November Direct Deposits	**56,167.21**
Less:	Bank Service Fee	**8.00**
	Errors and other items (list individually and explain):	
	Explanation	
Reconciled Balance per Checkbook at 11/30		**$ 25,600.48**

Exhibit 4.17a: The December Bank Statement

NCH Bank
1327 N Allen Place
Seattle, Washington 98117

The Park Cinema
415 Cedar Street
Seattle, WA 98121

Statement Date: 12/31/2010
Account # 45392

Account Summary:

Balance 11/30/2010	$29,954.19
Checks & Other Debits	-77,827.46
Deposits & Other Credits	76,717.55
Balance 12/31/2010	$28,844.28

Checks & Other Debits

2112	1-Dec	(288.75)
2118	2-Dec	(586.25)
NSF	3-Dec	(500.00)*
2117	3-Dec	(245.00)
2122	3-Dec	(674.12)
2120	6-Dec	(1,847.05)
2123	6-Dec	(1,200.00)
2125	6-Dec	(2,775.00)
2124	7-Dec	(4,056.00)
2127	9-Dec	(3,899.00)
2129	13-Dec	(1,089.75)
2132	13-Dec	(342.00)
2134	13-Dec	(473.50)
2136	13-Dec	(297.50)
2139	13-Dec	(369.00)
2128	14-Dec	(875.00)
2137	14-Dec	(603.75)
ATM	15-Dec	(500.00)
2130	16-Dec	(1,566.04)
2133	16-Dec	(533.75)
2138	16-Dec	(1,284.00)
2142	16-Dec	(36,000.00)
2131	17-Dec	(323.75)
2135	17-Dec	(486.00)
2140	17-Dec	(3,602.00)
2141	17-Dec	(2,650.00)
2143	20-Dec	(3,500.00)
2144	23-Dec	(3,465.00)
2147	27-Dec	(500.00)
2146	28-Dec	(160.00)
2148	28-Dec	(500.00)
2150	29-Dec	(236.25)
2151	29-Dec	(369.00)
2153	29-Dec	(472.50)
2156	29-Dec	(507.50)
2152	30-Dec	(420.00)
2155	30-Dec	(280.00)
2154	31-Dec	(342.00)
SC	31-Dec	(8.00)

Deposits & Other Credits

1-Dec	DEP	3,613.34
6-Dec	AD	23,186.73*
7-Dec	DEP	3,100.00
13-Dec	AD	13,384.60*
13-Dec	DEP	8,364.46
20-Dec	DEP	2,426.07
27-Dec	AD	19,574.29*
27-Dec	DEP	2,940.60
31-Dec	INT	127.46

KEY:	
AD	Automatic Deposit
ATM	Automatic Teller Machine
DEP	Deposit
INT	Interest Income
NSF	Insufficient funds
SC	Service Charge

*See *Exhibit 4.17b* for more details concerning these items.

The Park Cinema #2112
415 Cedar Street
Seattle, Washington
98121

Date 11/27/2010

Pay to the order of Dan Evans $ 288.75

NCH Bank-1327 N Allen Place, Seattle, Washington 98117

Memo ______________ Signature: Carlos Viga

1: 068674830¶45392¶2112

The Park Cinema #2122
415 Cedar Street
Seattle, Washington
98121

Date 12/1/2010

Pay to the order of NCH Bank $ 674.12

NCH Bank-1327 N Allen Place, Seattle, Washington 98117

Memo ______________ Signature: Carlos Viga

1: 068674830¶45392¶2122

The Park Cinema #2118
415 Cedar Street
Seattle, Washington
98121

Date 11/27/2010

Pay to the order of Pete Shkunatov $ 586.25

NCH Bank-1327 N Allen Place, Seattle, Washington 98117

Memo ______________ Signature: Carlos Viga

1: 068674830¶45392¶2118

NCH Bank December 31, 2010 Page 2 of 13

The Park Cinema
415 Cedar Street
Seattle, Washington
98121

#2117

Date 11/27/2010

Pay to the order of Heidi Moore $ 245.00

NCH Bank-1327 N Allen Place, Seattle, Washington 98117

Memo ______ Signature: Carlos Viga

1: 068674830¶45392¶2117

The Park Cinema
415 Cedar Street
Seattle, Washington
98121

#2120

Date 11/30/2010

Pay to the order of NWCS $ 1,847.05

NCH Bank-1327 N Allen Place, Seattle, Washington 98117

Memo ______ Signature: Carlos Viga

1: 068674830¶45392¶2120

The Park Cinema
415 Cedar Street
Seattle, Washington
98121

#2123

Date 12/4/2010

Pay to the order of Rock Construction $ 1,200 —

NCH Bank-1327 N Allen Place, Seattle, Washington 98117

Memo ______ Signature: Carlos Viga

1: 068674830¶45392¶2123

The Park Cinema #2125
415 Cedar Street
Seattle, Washington
98121
Date 12/4/2010

Pay to the order of NWCS $ 2,775 —

NCH Bank-1327 N Allen Place, Seattle, Washington 98117

Memo Signature: Carlos Vega

1: 068674830¶45392¶2125

The Park Cinema #2124
415 Cedar Street
Seattle, Washington
98121
Date 12/4/2010

Pay to the order of Premier Entertainment $ 4,056 —

NCH Bank-1327 N Allen Place, Seattle, Washington 98117

Memo Signature: Carlos Vega

1: 068674830¶45392¶2124

The Park Cinema #2127
415 Cedar Street
Seattle, Washington
98121
Date 12/4/2010

Pay to the order of Visa $ 3,899 —

NCH Bank-1327 N Allen Place, Seattle, Washington 98117

Memo Signature: Carlos Vega

1: 068674830¶45392¶2127

The Park Cinema #2129
415 Cedar Street Date 12/11/2010
Seattle, Washington
98121

Pay to the order of Precision Graphics $ 1,089.75

NCH Bank-1327 N Allen Place, Seattle, Washington 98117

Memo ______ Signature: Carlos Viga

1: 068674830¶45392¶2129

The Park Cinema #2132
415 Cedar Street Date 12/11/2010
Seattle, Washington
98121

Pay to the order of Don Guardia $ 342.00

NCH Bank-1327 N Allen Place, Seattle, Washington 98117

Memo ______ Signature: Carlos Viga

1: 068674830¶45392¶2132

The Park Cinema #2134
415 Cedar Street Date 12/11/2010
Seattle, Washington
98121

Pay to the order of Kristen Holtman $ 473.50

NCH Bank-1327 N Allen Place, Seattle, Washington 98117

Memo ______ Signature: Carlos Viga

1: 068674830¶45392¶2134

NCH Bank December 31, 2010 Page 5 of 13

The Park Cinema
415 Cedar Street
Seattle, Washington
98121

#2136

Date 12/1/2010

Pay to the order of Heidi Moore $ 297.50

NCH Bank-1327 N Allen Place, Seattle, Washington 98117

Memo ______________ Signature: Carlos Viga

1: 068674830¶45392¶2136

The Park Cinema
415 Cedar Street
Seattle, Washington
98121

#2139

Date 12/11/2010

Pay to the order of Will Tsai $ 369 —

NCH Bank-1327 N Allen Place, Seattle, Washington 98117

Memo ______________ Signature: Carlos Viga

1: 068674830¶45392¶2139

The Park Cinema
415 Cedar Street
Seattle, Washington
98121

#2128

Date 12/11/2010

Pay to the order of Seattle Public Utility $ 875 —

NCH Bank-1327 N Allen Place, Seattle, Washington 98117

Memo ______________ Signature: Carlos Viga

1: 068674830¶45392¶2128

NCH Bank December 31, 2010 Page 6 of 13

The Park Cinema #2137
415 Cedar Street Date 12/11/2010
Seattle, Washington
98121

Pay to the order of Pete Shkumatov $ 603.75

NCH Bank-1327 N Allen Place, Seattle, Washington 98117

Memo ______________ Signature: Carlos Viga

1: 068674830¶45392¶2137

The Park Cinema #2130
415 Cedar Street Date 12/11/2010
Seattle, Washington
98121

Pay to the order of NWCS $ 1,566.04

NCH Bank-1327 N Allen Place, Seattle, Washington 98117

Memo ______________ Signature: Carlos Viga

1: 068674830¶45392¶2130

The Park Cinema #2133
415 Cedar Street Date 12/11/2010
Seattle, Washington
98121

Pay to the order of Rick Hart $ 533.75

NCH Bank-1327 N Allen Place, Seattle, Washington 98117

Memo ______________ Signature: Carlos Viga

1: 068674830¶45392¶2133

NCH Bank December 31, 2010 Page 7 of 13

The Park Cinema #2138
415 Cedar Street Date 12/11/2010
Seattle, Washington
98121

Pay to the order of Matt Tenpil $ 1,284 —

NCH Bank-1327 N Allen Place, Seattle, Washington 98117

Memo ______ Signature: Carlos Viga

1: 068674830¶45392¶2138

The Park Cinema #2142
415 Cedar Street Date 12/15/2010
Seattle, Washington
98121

Pay to the order of Martin Howell $ 36,000 —

NCH Bank-1327 N Allen Place, Seattle, Washington 98117

Memo ______ Signature: Carlos Viga

1: 068674830¶45392¶2142

The Park Cinema #2131
415 Cedar Street Date 12/4/2010
Seattle, Washington
98121

Pay to the order of Dan Evans $ 323.75

NCH Bank-1327 N Allen Place, Seattle, Washington 98117

Memo ______ Signature: Carlos Viga

1: 068674830¶45392¶2131

NCH Bank December 31, 2010 Page 8 of 13

The Park Cinema #2135
415 Cedar Street Date 12/1/2010
Seattle, Washington
98121

Pay to the order of Luis Mejia $ 486.00

NCH Bank-1327 N Allen Place, Seattle, Washington 98117

Memo Signature: Carlos Viga

1: 068674830¶45392¶2135

The Park Cinema #2140
415 Cedar Street Date 12/13/2010
Seattle, Washington
98121

Pay to the order of Premier Entertainment $ 3,602 –

NCH Bank-1327 N Allen Place, Seattle, Washington 98117

Memo Solitary Man 12/1 – 12/11 Signature: Carlos Viga

1: 068674830¶45392¶2140

The Park Cinema #2141
415 Cedar Street Date 12/15/2010
Seattle, Washington
98121

Pay to the order of Seattle Times $ 2,650 –

NCH Bank-1327 N Allen Place, Seattle, Washington 98117

Memo Signature: Carlos Vega

1: 068674830¶45392¶2141

NCH Bank December 31, 2010 Page 9 of 13

The Park Cinema #2143
415 Cedar Street Date 12/15/2010
Seattle, Washington
98121

Pay to the order of KPLZ Radio $ 3,500 -

NCH Bank-1327 N Allen Place, Seattle, Washington 98117

Memo ______ Signature: Carlos Vega

1: 0686748300¶45392¶2143

The Park Cinema #2144
415 Cedar Street Date 12/21/2010
Seattle, Washington
98121

Pay to the order of Countrywide Cars. $ 3,465 -

NCH Bank-1327 N Allen Place, Seattle, Washington 98117

Memo ______ Signature: Carlos Vega

1: 0686748300¶45392¶2144

The Park Cinema #2147
415 Cedar Street Date 12/23/2010
Seattle, Washington
98121

Pay to the order of WS Youth Arts $ 500 -

NCH Bank-1327 N Allen Place, Seattle, Washington 98117

Memo ______ Signature: Carlos Vega

1: 0686748300¶45392¶2147

NCH Bank December 31, 2010 Page 10 of 13

The Park Cinema #2146
415 Cedar Street Date 12/23/2010
Seattle, Washington
98121

Pay to the order of Vasquez & Co $ 160 —

NCH Bank-1327 N Allen Place, Seattle, Washington 98117

Memo ________ Signature: Carlos Vega

1: 068674830¶45392¶2146

The Park Cinema #2148
415 Cedar Street Date 12/23/2010
Seattle, Washington
98121

Pay to the order of Seattle Conservatory $ 500 —

NCH Bank-1327 N Allen Place, Seattle, Washington 98117

Memo ________ Signature: Carlos Vega

1: 068674830¶45392¶2148

The Park Cinema #2150
415 Cedar Street Date 12/27/2010
Seattle, Washington
98121

Pay to the order of Dan Evans $ 236.25

NCH Bank-1327 N Allen Place, Seattle, Washington 98117

Memo ________ Signature: Carlos Vega

1: 068674830¶45392¶2150

NCH Bank December 31, 2010 Page 11 of 13

The Park Cinema
415 Cedar Street
Seattle, Washington
98121

#2151

Date 12/27/2010

Pay to the order of Don Guardia $ 369 —

NCH Bank-1327 N Allen Place, Seattle, Washington 98117

Memo

Signature: Carlos Vega

1: 068674830¶45392¶2151

The Park Cinema
415 Cedar Street
Seattle, Washington
98121

#2153

Date 12/27/2010

Pay to the order of Kristin Holtman $ 472.50

NCH Bank-1327 N Allen Place, Seattle, Washington 98117

Memo

Signature: Carlos Vega

1: 068674830¶45392¶2153

The Park Cinema
415 Cedar Street
Seattle, Washington
98121

#2156

Date 12/27/2010

Pay to the order of Pete Shkunatov $ 507.50

NCH Bank-1327 N Allen Place, Seattle, Washington 98117

Memo

Signature: Carlos Vega

1: 068674830¶45392¶2156

NCH Bank December 31, 2010 Page 12 of 13

The Park Cinema
415 Cedar Street
Seattle, Washington
98121

#2152

Date 12/27/2010

Pay to the order of Rick Hart $ 420 -

NCH Bank-1327 N Allen Place, Seattle, Washington 98117

Memo ______________ Signature: Carlos Viga

1: 068674830¶45392¶2152

The Park Cinema
415 Cedar Street
Seattle, Washington
98121

#2155

Date 12/27/2010

Pay to the order of Heidi Moore $ 280 -

NCH Bank-1327 N Allen Place, Seattle, Washington 98117

Memo ______________ Signature: Carlos Viga

1: 068674830¶45392¶2155

The Park Cinema
415 Cedar Street
Seattle, Washington
98121

#2154

Date 12/27/2010

Pay to the order of Luis Meijia $ 342 -

NCH Bank-1327 N Allen Place, Seattle, Washington 98117

Memo ______________ Signature: Carlos Viga

1: 068674830¶45392¶2154

NCH Bank December 31, 2010 Page 13 of 13

Exhibit 4.17b: Details of Items Noted in December Bank Statement (*Exhibit 4.17a*)

I. NSF

This check was received in late November from Shameless Boutique for its November OSA. When NCH Bank presented this check to Shameless Boutique's bank, it was notified that the check could not be honored due to insufficient funds available in Shameless Boutique's account. Accordingly, the check has been noted on the December bank statement as NSF (insufficient funds).

II. Breakdown of Automatic Deposits (AD) made in December by Debit & Credit Card Companies

DEBIT CARD PURCHASES			
Deposit Date	Bank Deposit	3% Service Fee	Total Customer Charge
Monday, December 6	$8,497.11	$262.80	$8,759.91
Monday, December 13	4,790.22	148.15	4,938.37
Monday, December 27	6,860.70	212.19	7,072.89
	$ 20,148.03	$623.14	$20,771.17
CREDIT CARD PURCHASES			
Deposit Date	Bank Deposit	3% Service Fee	Total Customer Charge
Monday, December 6	$ 14,689.62	$ 454.32	$15,143.94
Monday, December 13	8,594.38	265.81	8,860.19
Monday, December 27	12,713.59	393.20	13,106.79
	$35,997.59	$1,113.33	$ 37,110.92
Grand Total	$56,145.62	$1,736.47	$57,882.09